IN PRAISE OF JANA SIPE BERNDT'S

Finding Norm

Finding Norm is a bravely honest telling of the kind of grief and loss no one should have to endure. Yet Jana somehow manages to turn her story into a page-turner, inviting the reader into her pain, her joy, and her transformative faith. As Jana works to find her new Norm, there's something here for everyone: understanding and solidarity for those who grieve, and insight and wisdom for those who long to better care for their grieving loved ones. Wherever you are on your journey, this is a book you don't want to pass up.

REV. JEN TYLER, *Contributing Editor,*
We Pray with Her: Encouragement For All Women Who Lead

Jana's transparency invites us on a journey of remembering, laughter, and gratitude. Loss is inevitable, but how we respond can lead us to joy. *Finding Norm* will bring solace and comfort to your soul.

DAVE KINSMAN, *Author, Hope Has Arrived*

"Widow" was not a word I wanted to be associated with, nor was it part of my personal life plan. In *Finding Norm,* Jana opens the door to self discovery: Although my new title is unwelcome, it unfolds to a different plan.

COLETTE BARTON, *Widow, Executive Director of Richland-Wilkin United Way*

Throughout her journey of hope after devastating loss, Jana candidly shares how *true* faith in God gives strength and opportunity to move forward. For those who have endured the challenge of grief, Jana guides with tears, humor, and gratitude to finding *our* "Norm" along with J-O-Y for a new forever.

MARCIA RICHMAN, *Licensed Social Worker*

Jana's ability to peel away the layers of defensiveness to tell an honest story of her encounter with grief is a rare talent. Her story of resiliency gives hope to all who have encountered life-changing adversity and uplifts the broken-hearted through truth, honesty, and realism.

DIANE CORDES, *School Superintendent, Masters in Counseling Psychology*

Finding Norm is a love story. Written with simplicity, charity, grace and wit, Jana Sipe Berndt chronicles the events that rocked the very foundation of her being. Suddenly widowed, she is faced with the task of raising three young adult children while crawling in the darkness of her grief. With courage and faith, she arises and walks into the light, "finding Norm."

Finding Norm: Rediscovering Joy through a Season of Loss gives us permission to grieve in our own ways and, most importantly, to be gentle with ourselves.

FATHER JIM CALLAHAN, *Pastor of St. Mary's, Worthington MN*

As the niece who walked alongside her and witnessed her growth, I observed this amazing story, which showcases Jana Sipe Berndt's relentless faith and incredible road to healing. *Finding Norm* is a book for our seasons of loss, a testimony that even as our "norm" may change, God's love and faithfulness never will.

ANNA LEIGH LESNAR, *Elementary Teacher*

Finding Norm

REDISCOVERING JOY THROUGH A SEASON OF LOSS

Jana Sipe Berndt

Finding Norm
Rediscovering Joy Through a Season of Loss

By Jana Sipe Berndt

Published by:
RWR Press

Soft Cover ISBN: 978-1-7332297-0-8
Hard Cover ISBN: 978-1-7332297-1-5

Library of Congress Number: 2019908182

Cover design by Kathryn Lesnar, Worthington MN
Cover photo by LeMar Photography, Wahpeton ND
Layout design by Kate Pelzel, Worthington MN
Edited by Carol McAdoo Rehme
Printed by Bang Printing, St. Cloud MN.

Printed in the United States of America

www.janasipeberndt.com | jana@janasipeberndt.com

This book is inspired and dedicated to Randy W. Berndt -

my loving husband and best friend,
dedicated father, caring son, brother, uncle,
teacher, coach, mentor, friend and,
most of all, child of God.
Until we meet again . . . long live your memory.

Contents

· ·

Grief is the price you
pay for love.

~ QUEEN ELIZABETH II

The Collapse

EXPERIENCING LOSS

One

"*Norm!*"
A familiar name called out in harmony at a famous bar in Boston. *"Where everybody knows your name."* – Cheers.

Norm was a television character played by George Wendt on "Cheers," a popular 1980s TV show. Time and time again loveable Norm, a regular at the bar, was heckled by Sam, Carla, Rebecca, and all his other friends at Cheers. Without fail, he visited Cheers every day, rain or shine.

Norm was predictable, reliable, and loyal to *his* bar stool. He was routine. He was someone you could count on. He was comfortable and likeable. He represented the "norm."

Norm was my husband Randy's favorite character on the show, and for years it was our nightly ritual to watch "Cheers" after the ten o'clock news. It was our routine. It was *our* norm and it felt good.

Normal is a word that feels good to me most of the time and I believe most people—if they had a choice—would choose to live a normal life. A life that's comfortable, predictable, usual. Change is not bad. I enjoy experiencing new things. Yet I desire stability.

But when you're thrown a curve ball, unexpected and harsh, life becomes unpredictable and uncomfortable. Normal is tossed out the window.

The Merriam-Webster dictionary defines normal as "conforming to a standard, usual, typical, or expected."

Words like customary, predictable, expected are all part of a "normal" life.

For years, my husband and I thrived on a routine that was comfortable and pleasurable despite the changes we encountered: babies, new jobs, illness, and unexpected twists and turns.

· · · · · · ·

Randy and I created our fulfilling life in a small, western Minnesota town. With a scanty 3,500 people, Breckenridge was a place "where everybody knows your name." Our union produced three beautiful children and a loving twenty-eight years of marriage. We thrived in fulfilling careers: Randy taught school and coached; I was a banker. Rich in friends and family, we hosted backyard barbeques to enjoy their company. We invested in a recreational speedboat that delighted our children as well as our church family.

Life was good.

We had high hopes, happy events, and new dreams to realize in the near future. The excitement of our daughter's impending wedding. The joy of our son's graduation from high school. The uncharted thrills of empty-nesting. The dangling carrots of travel, grandchildren, wintering in the south.

Life was joyful.

With so much to plan and live for, we were the flesh-and-bone definition of normality. Our family wasn't Norman Rockwellpicture-perfect, but it felt pretty darn close.

But, suddenly, unexpectedly, Norm was no longer on his barstool.

My Randy died.

Two

Outside my opened window, a brilliant autumn morning teased me with the earthy scent of crisp, dried leaves under wide blue skies. Ignoring the temptation, I stretched my back into the yoga Child's Pose, faithfully following my morning routine.

When the phone rang, I glanced at the clock. *Who calls at 8:30 on a Sunday morning?*

It was a friend, Bruce. His voice was tentative. "Hey, Jana, is Randy out running with the dog?"

I paused before answering. Oddly, my husband hadn't woken me before he left that day, but it was reasonable to assume he was out doing the thing he loved.

I shrugged. "Uh, probably."

"Well, I think it might be Randy and Max out on Highway 210." Bruce hesitated. "It looks like he might, uh, need a little help."

My heart rate increased a bit. "Help? What kind of help?"

"An ambulance was just arriving. And I could see police caring for Randy and the dog," Bruce said, "but I figured you would want to know."

My stomach tightened a tad.

Darting through the house, I woke Matthew and told him to get dressed because we needed to help his dad. Though I moved quickly, I didn't feel panicked. I pictured a simple injury. A sprained ankle, a broken leg, something relatively minor but bad enough that he couldn't manage without help.

It wasn't until we approached the scene on the highway that I realized this was much more than a runner who had a small issue.

Emergency lights blazed. The ambulance, buttoned tight, was ready to pull away. Max sat alone in a locked police car, his snout pressed against the window.

Where was Randy?

Where was the officer?

I looked around helplessly.

Suddenly frightened and desperate for answers, I approached a familiar-looking couple sitting nearby in their pickup. "Is Randy in the ambulance?"

The expressions on their faces told me the answer before they even responded.

My heart thumped and nausea swept over me. Somehow, I summoned the sensibility to check my cell phone app and see that Randy's Fitbit revealed his last step on Highway 210 was at 8:06 a.m. It was now 8:45.

So many unanswered questions. How long had he been out? What had happened? Was it as serious as it felt? Was he still breathing? Was he …?

Although the hospital was in view and only a few minutes away, the drive felt like hours. Matthew and I watched as they lifted my lifeless husband from the back of the ambulance and wheeled him into the ER. I had never been so scared in all my life.

What was going to happen to him? To us? To our family?

A young receptionist greeted us and escorted us directly to a family waiting room near the ER. Her nervousness was obvious. Had the EMTs called ahead and prepped her? Did she know something? Were they going to be able to save him? Had they already pronounced him dead?

Within a short time, a hospital chaplain arrived to assist my son and me through the next intensely stressful moments. She talked to us, prayed with us, and tried to comfort us as we waited for answers.

By now, we had learned that Randy wasn't transported for an ankle injury or broken bones but something much more serious. Had he collapsed for some reason? Or had a heart attack? Possibly, I supposed. But my healthy husband had no previous history of problematic issues. I was stymied.

And worried.

Please be alive please be alive please be alive. The prayer was a litany that I breathed repeatedly. The mother in me wanted to reassure Matthew. But the wife in me feared the worst.

So consumed with my dread, I had forgotten about other important people. My brain slowly began registering where I was and what I needed to do. Our other two children needed to know what was happening.

I made a few phones calls but wasn't able to reach Emily, who was in her junior year of college in Nashville, Tennessee. When I reached her fiancé, Mitchell, he promised to have her call me as soon as possible.

After several attempts, I finally connected with my oldest son, Tyler.

"I'll leave right away for Breckenridge, Mom," he said. It would be an emotionally fraught four-hour drive from Minneapolis where he lived and worked, but he promised to arrive as soon as he could.

My mind swirled with such emotion, panic, and fear that I couldn't think straight. What should I do next? Who else should I call? Friends? Church? Pastor?

As we sat waiting to hear something, anything, I reflected on Randy's health and wracked my brain about any possible warning signs that something was wrong with him.

Randy had just finished his eighth year coaching both boys' and girls' cross country teams at Breckenridge High. Toward the end of the fall season he had, I recalled, experienced a bit of fatigue.

I suddenly remembered a day—Was it last week? The week before? —when he came home from practice saying, "I just couldn't run with the team today. I was too tired."

He had come to get his bike so that day he could keep up with his runners. Although it was odd, I hadn't thought much about it.

Now I wondered: *Had that been a warning sign?*

Randy and I had easily dismissed the incident, deciding he had been teaching all day, not eaten a good lunch, was probably hungry, maybe a little dehydrated.

Waiting now for the doctor to give me answers, I reflected on the morning. Why had Randy left for a run without telling me? Was he testing himself? Checking his stamina? Was this something as innocent as fatigue or was there an underlying issue?

In the sterile, quiet family room we continued to wait and pray. After sitting so long, I excused myself and headed toward the restroom. As I approached the nurse's station, I overheard someone frantically yell, "We've lost him!"

I froze.

Not my Randy! He's healthy. He's vibrant and active. He's a runner. He's too young. I'm too young to be a widow. He's ... he's ....

Please, God, not Randy.

I turned and slowly retraced my steps to the waiting room to be with Matthew, who was alone with the hospital chaplain, Barb. She tried to comfort us through our shock and devastation.

I realized I should take a few minutes to reach out to a

few friends, alert them to our situation, and ask for their prayers. I contacted John and Marcia, who would want to know. Oh, and Kent and Annette who expected me to be at church soon to play piano with the band. All of them raced to my side, waiting with us for an update, a word about Randy's condition, a diagnosis. Anything.

We prayed urgently together and tried to stay hopeful as we waited for news from the medical team.

Together, a doctor and nurse finally approached us.

"Your husband has had a heart attack." The ER doctor's demeanor was kind but grave as he explained Randy's condition.

My thoughts raced along with my pounding heart. But I knew I needed to keep myself together for the sake of my son.

A "widow-maker" he called it, a term foreign to me. So swift and massive is this particularly deadly type of heart attack, few survive. Hence its descriptive, awful, literal name: widow-maker.

Somehow—miraculously—they had revived and stabilized Randy.

He's alive! Praise the Lord, Randy's alive!

"But," cautioned the doctor, "we need to transport him to Fargo for further care."

Fargo? I could handle Fargo. Anything, anywhere, as long as Randy was still alive. "Can we see him?"

The nurse escorted Matthew and me deep into the ER. I was totally unprepared for what came next.

My husband lay—unresponsive—on the hospital bed. Intimidating wires, machines, loud noises, and nurses were everywhere. But I could see color in his cheeks and his eyes fluttered a bit as if to assure, "I know you're here."

Our friend Bob, the nurse anesthetist, adjusted Randy for comfort as he explained, "He'll be airlifted to Sanford Hospital for heart surgery."

Heart surgery? As scary as that sounded, I could handle heart surgery. Anything, as long as it kept Randy alive and gave us a long, full life together. Sure, heart surgery would be the answer.

The rest of the world slipped away as—in shock and disbelief—I focused my thoughts and attention on my husband. Staff continued to stabilize and prepare him for the transfer. He seemed to slip in and out of consciousness. When Bob assured me that Randy could hear me, I approached his bed. I calmed somewhat when I felt the warmth of his body and sensed that he did not know where he was or what had just happened.

I reached for his hand. Talked to him. Tried to reassure him. His eyes opened and closed a few times, seemingly in response to my questions and voice.

I leaned closer. "I'm here, Randy. Matthew is here, too. You've had a heart attack but it's going to be okay."

There was hope in my voice. And, deep in my heart, I believed what I said.

Everything would be okay.

Three

Within thirty minutes, we all headed north. Randy in the helicopter, Matthew and I in our Buick Enclave with Kent, who generously offered to drive. This all-so-familiar road, taken without thought many times for shopping sprees and dinner dates at our favorite restaurants, was suddenly an agonizing, lengthy forty-five-minute trek.

While Kent expertly manned the steering wheel, I called Randy's brother Steven, an anesthesiologist on staff at Sanford, who agreed to meet us at the hospital. As the countryside blurred by, my mind ran laps around the track.

Would Randy really be okay? What would we find when we got to the hospital? Was he already in surgery? Would he survive the surgery?

I felt my earlier optimism fade as fear grabbed hold.

Steven arrived about the same time we did. He gave me a quick hug before heading to the surgery wing, leaving his wife

Darlene with us. I was comforted to know Steven would be with Randy and could explain the medical procedure in layman's terms.

The lobby began filling with Randy's cheer team. Marcia, John, and Annette had followed us into Fargo, along with other family and close friends who came to support us.

Although still dazed, I thought to call Emily with an update and Tyler to let him know we were all in Fargo. Oh, and my parents who were wintering in Florida. Steven had already made a few calls to Randy's other siblings and their stepmom Shirley—asking for their fervent prayers.

"Hang tight," we told everyone. "We'll keep in touch as we learn more."

Tyler, well on his way to Fargo, would arrive shortly. The others wanted to meet us there, too, but I encouraged them to hold off. "Let's just wait and see," I said, having no idea what the next few days would bring.

Dressed in scrubs, Steven entered the lobby. He had been with the surgeon who performed a procedure on Randy. He updated us and explained the procedure they had done on his heart. Randy had several stents put in, but there appeared to have been a long period of time that he was without oxygen, which causes swelling and potential damage to the brain. The plan was to put Randy into a medically induced coma to cool his body and allow time for the brain swelling to go down, which would also give his heart time to begin to heal.

Randy had made it this far. He was alive. He would rest and heal.

Relief seeped through me and I took the first deep breath I'd had since doing my yoga. *Was that really this morning? So much has happened since then.*

I soaked up the stillness of the moment. Rest. That's what we all needed for few days.

Be still and rest.

Four

So the waiting began.

Monday was a peaceful, restful day of family and close friends coming and going from Randy's private room. We settled near his bed, close enough to hold his hand and talk to him. We reminisced and shared "Randy stories" with the nurses and other medical staff who made their way in and out of the room all day. I needed these complete strangers to know and care about this wonderful man who was a father, teacher, mentor, coach, and so much more.

Dr. Siep and Dr. Harms, the internal medicine doctors assigned to Randy's case, stopped in several times to update us on their plan to keep him quiet and still—in a medically induced coma—for another day or so, which somehow eased my anxiousness. Perhaps this was my body's way of taking a break from the seriousness of his condition. Or it was my denial of all that was happening to and around us.

The night shift change introduced us to a new nurse, Jacob,

with his friendly, calming demeanor. We were surprised to learn he was a former student of Randy's who "met Mr. Berndt in a different way."

Jacob had been an eighth grader when Randy got his first teaching job in Fargo. Jacob told us he was a broken-hearted kid, mourning the recent loss of his dad. Randy became the compassionate teacher who guided him through a turbulent school year. His story jarred a faint memory, and I recalled how Randy—young and inexperienced—had strived his best to help the middle schooler grieve.

The topic of conversation in the crammed ICU room changed and we stumbled upon another blessed coincidence: running. Jacob, it turned out, was a runner, a good runner, a former cross-country runner at Fargo South High. As a bonus, he was quite tall, like Randy, and an Asics shoe loyalist—another passion they had in common. To make this small world even smaller, he had ran cross-country in high school with a teammate of Tyler's at Saint John's University. After making this final connection, we were comforted with that knowledge that this was *more than* mere coincidence; God had placed Jacob there that night, reconnecting him with Randy.

Tyler journaled onto the CaringBridge website:

JOURNAL ENTRY BY TYLER BERNDT
OCTOBER 27, 2014

Because all good things come in threes, Jacob and I put two and two together and discovered my dad was his eighth grade algebra teacher. He made it through high school, college, and has a sweet job at Sanford so I'm saying some of that algebra knowledge paid off. I plan to make flashcards to quiz him in the morning after his twelve-hour shift—just to test that theory.

It's a funny thing about runners—they have a way of sticking together, even in the weirdest of situations. I have no idea what the future will bring, but I have no doubt there are no hands I'd rather have Dad in, nor hands that he'd rather be in, than those of a runner.

From my perch next to Randy, I calmed as I watched his chest expand in rhythm to the machines.

He has to be okay. We've made it this far, right?

Reassurance accompanied me home that night. I felt peace knowing Randy was in the care of his student, a student placed in Randy's life and now ours with divine intension.

Five

Tuesday dawned quickly. When I returned to the hospital, I was surprised to learn nurse Jacob had had a difficult night with Randy in ICU. His seizure-type activity was a grave concern, spurring an early visit from the medical team who updated me on Randy's condition.

"There appears to have been some brain damage," said Dr. Siep. "Probably due to a loss of oxygen."

Brain damage? Brain damage! Surely not ….

I found the courage to ask, "How much?"

"We won't know until we do a scan of his brain."

Although Dr. Siep had hoped to wait a few days, I sensed his anxiousness to find out sooner rather than later. By moving up the test, he felt they could get a better sense of what they were dealing with.

Somewhat reluctantly, I agreed to the necessary electroencephalogram (EEG) and a magnetic resonance image

(MRI) if needed to determine how much—if any—damage there might be.

I clung to the *if any.*

A slow, deliberate process began to bring Randy out of his medically induced coma by warming his body. By Tuesday afternoon, it was time: They would bring him to consciousness.

We all waited. And not patiently. It seemed to take forever. But after an hour or so, they summoned us.

This was it.

This was the moment we had been waiting for. The results of the EEG and MRI.

Had the lack of oxygen hurt him? Was this all going to work itself out?

As a united front, Team Randy assembled for the news. Ignoring my earlier phone counsel to sit tight, Emily had responded firmly, "He's my daddy. I'm coming home now." She and Mitchell, like her brother Tyler, had arrived Sunday evening to find their dad in a coma. As devastating as it was for them, now I was glad, strengthened by having all my children present. Together we could handle this.

The waiting room near the ICU where Randy "slept" was small and tight, public yet intimate. Squeezed next to us were his brothers and stepmother, along with my brother-in-law and nieces, who wanted to see and hear the results firsthand.

The neurologist, along with Dr. Siep and Dr. Harms, showed us Randy's brain scans.

"The damage was extensive." The neurologist paused to let his weighty words sink in. "The length of time your husband was without oxygen was just too much for his brain to withstand."

Perhaps lying on the highway or perhaps en route to Fargo or perhaps in surgery or ... somewhere ... along the way, Randy had suffered several strokes. The combined loss of oxygen was ... deadly.

The brain damage was severe. It had robbed him of his

eyesight. He was blind. The area of the brain that controlled emotions and personality was hit especially hard.

The Randy I married and loved with all my heart was gone. My husband would not survive.

No!

How could this be?

Was it a mistake? Had Randy's scan gotten switched with someone else's? Maybe the EEG machine hadn't worked properly? Was there some other, more accurate, test?

There was nothing to be done, the doctor told us. Nothing could repair the damage. Nothing could bring Randy back.

Like lifeblood dripping away, I felt the hope I had mustered and nurtured during the past few days drain from me.

I was crushed.

Devastated.

My *Norm* was gone.

Six

I did the only thing I could do. I sobbed.

My husband was going to die.

My heart was crushed and for a minute I wanted my life to be over, too. I could not have imagined any worse news than what the neurologist had just shared.

I wanted to wake up and have someone tell me this was just all a bad dream. A horrible nightmare.

The nightmare did not end and I did not wake to any better news. This was real. What I had heard was the truth.

Clinging to each other, we left the waiting room and found a crowd in the hallway, more family and friends anxious to hear the outcome of the tests. I didn't have the energy—or the will—to share the devastating news, but I could see that our faces confirmed their worst fears. They knew from our shock and still-flowing tears that Randy's future was bleak.

Unable to bear the sympathy of others so soon, I whirled

around and rushed back to Randy's side. I needed to hold his hand again, to feel his heart beat. To gather the strength necessary to help my children process the medical findings.

Maybe God would take this all away and send us a sudden miracle. Randy would wake up and be all right. I clung to that hope.

The kids joined me, and we spent the evening next to Randy, praying, talking to him, listening to some of his favorite worship music. A sacred calmness seeped into me as I sat next to his bed, holding his warm hand and feeling his pulse as we touched.

But, deep down, my insides were in a knot.

So much grief. So many decisions waiting to be made. Heavy hearted, I dragged myself from the hospital late that night, my mind weighty and worried.

What was next? What was going to happen? How could I maneuver through this ordeal?

It was all too much for my tired brain to handle.

I couldn't think straight. I knew I needed sleep and some alone time to process the day, the news, and the future. A fractured future I never imagined possible.

The kids and I were on the hills and in the valleys of disbelief and utter sadness. We found ourselves in the throes of unstoppable tears, occasional laughter, and utter silence—our emotions were an unpredictable, scary rollercoaster ride with no one manning the control lever.

Seven

Wednesday began before sunrise when—rested from a surprisingly decent night's sleep at Steve and Darlene's—I headed determinedly to the hospital to see what medical decisions I would be asked to consider.

It turned out there were many decisions to be made.

Dr. Siep and Dr. Harms checked in that morning to see if I had any questions they could answer. Deep down I knew they were waiting for me to settle The Big Decision:

Keep Randy on life support?

Or … take him off life support?

I posed question after question with the same theme.

Are you sure we've tried everything to save his life?

Isn't there any more medicine to try?

How about another test, just to make sure?

Or maybe time be my answer, we just needed more time to pass, for Randy to heal, to get better.

Dr. Siep was a kind soul who had a strong connection to Randy's brother Steven. They spent some of their early medical career together and had reconnected after years apart. He spoke frankly: "Our job as your doctors is to tell you the truth. We have done everything we can to save him. We know of no more medical tests or interventions that will change the outcome. Jana, there is nothing more we can do for Randy."

He was doing his best to be patient with me, and I could sense from his tone of voice and the nervousness in his posture how much he wanted me to make the ultimate decision.

"Time is of the essence, Jana. You really need to decide what you think is best. But, if you intend to donate Randy's organs, your decision needs to be made sooner rather than later."

Donate his organs?

Wait! I didn't know this was under consideration. Harvesting … transplanting …. I was still praying for a miracle and the doctors were talking transplantation?

The world was spinning and I was at a standstill. *Please, I prayed, give me time to sit with him for a while. Just a little longer. Please.*

"I … I just can't go there yet. I'm not ready to think about …."

Dr. Siep interrupted. "It's okay, Jana. Really, you only need to make one choice at this point: on or off life support."

Period. That was it.

The agonizing decision was mine to make. As much as I wanted it to be a group decision, I knew legally it had to come from Randy's wife, me. The entire weight fell on my shoulders.

Accepting this unwanted news was difficult and we each had individual steps to take in owning it. I recognized that the kids and I were at different places in processing and accepting that Randy was never going to be Randy again. Tyler, much like his dad, was the research person of the family and had already read numerous articles about organ donation. He suggested we meet with a nonprofit group, LifeSource, to learn about our options.

I found myself reluctant but willing to listen, if only for Tyler's sake. Matthew seemed agreeable to the conversation, mostly because he trusted the advice of his older brother. Emily, however, was still in the mindset that her dad was going to get better and God would take all of this away from us. She had no interest in consulting with the team, no interest in hearing what they had to say. She wasn't ready.

Nervously, reluctantly, we met with LifeSource representatives, Steven and Darlene at our sides.

LifeSource (a nonprofit organization dedicated to saving lives through organ, eye, and tissue donation) knew their facts and were professionally trained to handle a family like ours. They provided warm care and guidance as I slowly began considering the options for Randy.

I was startled to learn that the decision wasn't mine to make, after all.

My dear husband, always a giver, forever helping others, had taken things into his own hands. On his State of Minnesota driver's license, Randy had—sometime in the past and unbeknownst to me—"checked the box," and chosen to be a donor.

It was so like him. Selfless and heroic.

But, wait a minute. Was the decision really made? Someone still had to decide *when* to remove life support. That ultimate responsibility loomed over me.

By now I had learned enough to know that successful donation was a matter of timing, before any deterioration took place.

If or when I choose to make that decision, then LifeSource may or may not be part of the process, I agonized.

So much pressure and it felt like so little time to decide. I shook my head in despair. What to do? On or off?

Steven! I thought. He worked daily in the medical world and I respected his education and experience. *He will know what's best for his own brother, right?*

When we talked, Steven admitted how he, too, had been praying and hoping for a miracle, for Randy to be healed. But that was before the brain scans, when he was still hopeful, with a strong faith that Randy could survive.

"The neurology results were crushing, Jana." Steven heaved a sigh. "I knew Randy would not and could not return to us as we knew and loved him."

"What do I do now, Steven?"

"That's one of the most painful questions I've ever been asked." After a long pause, he added, "But the choice is yours and your alone, Jana. I can't make it for you."

I felt a strong need to have my extended support team near me before I made this life-determining decision. My parents were on their way from Florida and my sister Kathy was traveling from Bosnia where she was on a mission trip—all of them scheduled to arrive later that day. I would wait for them.

In reality, I was still giving God time for a miracle. You know, like in the scriptures. *The Bible* talks about miracles Jesus performed. Especially the story about Lazarus. Where Christ raised him from the dead and brought him back to life.

And what about others Jesus healed from grave illnesses? If He did it then, would He maybe do it here, for Randy? Perhaps we just need to wait a little longer. We just needed to pray. And be still.

It's God's timing, not ours, I repeated over and over in my mind.

But even with my prayers, Steven's prayers, the kids' prayers, the prayers of so many friends and family, Randy waking up—I was beginning to see—wasn't to be the miracle of our story.

If ... if my husband isn't coming back to life, I pondered, *could we still do something with his life?*

So the rubber started to meet the road. My parents and sister arrived that afternoon. No more excuses; it was time.

Because my daughter still was not ready for this finality, Dr.

Harms asked if she could meet privately with Emily. We had grown close to this caring doctor over the past three days, and Emily trusted her.

They returned twenty minutes later.

"Mom, I don't want dad to die." Emily's voice caught. "But I don't want to make the decision for him either. I want you to make the decision for him and I will support whatever you decide."

It was at that moment I fully realized the responsibility was mine. Not Tyler's or Matthew's. Not Emily's. Not Steven's. Not the doctors or nurses. Mine and mine alone.

And, oh, did I feel alone.

At 3:30 p.m. I made the tortured choice to remove Randy from life support as soon as they could get the organ transplant process in place. As painful as this was, I felt a sweeping sense of relief.

Four days of agonized waiting. Over.

This weighty decision meant movement. Movement toward the next step. Movement forward.

Oddly, even as I waited for the nightmare to end, I didn't want it to be over because … because as long as I was in the nightmare, Randy was still alive. I could hold his hand. I could talk to him. I could see him and pray with him.

Pray over him.

Eight

Thursday bulged with a battery of tests and medical procedures, all prepping Randy's body and organs for the transplant procedure. When I could no longer bear to watch, I would excuse myself to take a walk to the waiting room—where I was reminded that life existed beyond the cardiac ICU. I would visit for a bit before returning to Randy's side.

I was introduced to a new medical provider, a nurse who helped families such as mine by creating keepsakes of their loved one's fingerprints. Darlene, who knew of this woman's ministry at the hospital, had made special arrangements for her to meet with me. I watched as she delicately formed the clay-type molds.

"I will take these clay impressions," she kindly explained, "and then transfer them to metal discs. Then those can be made into jewelry, remembrance pieces."

Pointer finger … thumb … Randy's ring finger. His wedding ring finger, followed by my wedding ring finger—an extra special imprint that would be transformed into a cherished treasure.

Necklace, keychain and dog collar charm for our family, all etched with Randy's prints.

His thumb on Emily, giving her guidance and support. Pointer fingers for Matthew and Tyler, showing the way— and for Max, also the pointer to keep him on the right path.

For me, there would be a necklace charm with his thumbprint on one side and his ring finger alongside mine on the other side. A talisman. A token. A touchstone to give me a feeling of connection to Randy, a connection as strong as an electric shock letting me know he was with me even in death.

• • • • • • • •

That same day, Sanford Hospital and LifeSource honored Randy with a special flag raising ceremony.

Encouraged by them to invite others, we posted the time on our CaringBridge web page. When the kids and I walked down the stairs from ICU to the hospital lobby, the crowd that met us took our breath away. Hundreds of friends, family, and community members arrived to witness and share this experience with us.

Students.

Athletes.

Former co-workers.

High school classmates.

The crowd filled the chilly yet sunny memorial gardens and beyond.

Our friend John walked at my side, shielding me from television cameras and curious onlookers. Pastor Bill provided some thoughts and a touching tribute to Randy.

Huddled together for warmth, each family member, in turn, cranked the large LifeSource flag upward—along with the medical team who took time to join us. Our talented friend Kent played a favorite hymn, "It Is Well with My Soul" on his flugelhorn as the flag climbed its way up the tall flagpole in front of the hospital entry.

A banner of giving, the LifeSource flag would fly between the American and the North Dakota state flag until Randy's donation was complete.

Nine

Friday was grueling and heartbreaking. Family members, friends, nurses, and doctors came to say their farewells. Randy's siblings and stepmother, my brothers, nieces, and nephews filtered in and out of Randy's room throughout the day.

At times, watching the devastation of others was so excruciating that I rushed from the room. At one point, I selfishly asked people to give me some space; I wanted, I needed time alone to simply sit with Randy and my thoughts.

The kids and I spent as much time as we could together with Randy, holding his hand, talking to him, and gaining strength from each other as we began our own goodbyes.

By afternoon, LifeSource had the arrangements in place. With sensitivity and dignity, they informed us that matches had been found and transplant teams were en route to harvest Randy's organs.

Now that we knew the end was near, every moment was precious. The night was long but the morning came way too soon.

As the Saturday sun began to lighten the morning sky, doubts flooded me.

Had I waited long enough for God to perform His miracle?

What if this was a test of faith or patience?

What if Randy rallied and started to wake?

Then, God gave me a gift.

Up to this point, Randy had been on five different anti-seizure medicines, a combination that kept his brain activity and seizures in check. Yet, suddenly, he began having noticeable seizure activity. I rushed into the ICU hallway and asked the nurses to help him.

Please, I prayed, *help the seizures stop. Please, God, I can't bear to see my husband this way.*

A doctor arrived and explained that Randy's seizures were breaking through his medications and there was nothing more to offer him. The seizures would happen more frequently.

"Eventually, Jana, your husband won't respond at all. It's just a matter of time."

I saw this as a sign from God, as if He were saying, "My child, you are making the right decision. Let Me take it from here."

At last, a serene, comforting peace swept over me and I was reassured that this was out of my hands and in God's.

By 7:00 a.m. the transplant team, surgeons, and medical team were ready.

The kids and I slipped into scrubs along with Steven and Darlene, my dad, and sister Kathy. In spite of my best efforts, I couldn't suppress the turmoil in my stomach. The knot hardened and grew. I was uncertain and scared.

We did what felt best at that moment: We held hands and prayed for God's peace, love, and comfort. I found myself silently pleading, *Lord, if this is a bad dream, could You please wake me up? Now!*

In a fog, I braced myself in the hallway where we stood while the team readied the surgical unit. I looked at the closed oversized door. On the other side, doctors were busy removing machines and life support aids that had sustained my husband to this point. *Will he be alive when we enter, or* .... The thought was too harsh to finish.

The unknown loomed just beyond. The knot in my belly twisted tighter. My knees turned to rubber and I felt as though I might collapse into a heap right there on the floor.

Once again doubt reared its insistent head.

Am I doing the right thing? I wondered for the umpteenth time. *Should we wait for* ...

The doors swept open.

My eyes scanned the dim, sterile room where medical equipment stood shoulder-to-shoulder, the eyes of doctors and nurses peered kindly above their mouth masks, and surgical tools lay, even and precise, at the ready for their part in the harvest. At the center of it all was Randy.

Prone on the table.

No wires or tubes connecting him to cumbersome machines. Just … Randy. Peacefully breathing on his own.

And then I heard it: music!

Soothing and sacred, the familiar soft strains of worship songs—playing somewhere in the background—sifted through me.

The profound peacefulness and quiet stillness of my husband calmed me.

It's going to be okay Jana, I felt him say.

We were guided to Randy's side. I reached for his hand and hugged him.

Each of the kids took a turn to embrace their dad, to say offer final words of love. And my dad, Kathy, Steven, Darlene … me … until the Doctor gave a nod as though to say, "He's gone."

We swiftly headed toward the door, but the Doctor summoned us back. We had misread the cue.

I gasped for air and felt a wave of faintness overcome me. Randy wasn't gone?

What was this?

A sign from God?

As we huddled again around Randy's bed, praying and talking softly to him, I saw on the monitor that his breathing was becoming faint and all of his vitals were dropping.

God whispered to my heart: *Jana, Randy is waiting for you to release him into My loving arms."*

I was not prepared for the words He placed on my lips and spoke through me: "It's okay, Randy. You can go and be with your mom and dad. We love you and we'll miss you, but we'll be okay."

Randy's gift to us was a slight release of his eyelids, followed by a single tear running down his cheek.

He had heard me. He knew we were there. He knew we loved him.

And he knew I was going to be okay.

Saturday, November 1, 2014, at 9:05 a.m., Randy Berndt took his last earthly breath. Surrounded by his devoted family and medical team, he crossed the threshold to his heavenly home.

Ten

JOURNAL ENTRY BY JANA BERNDT
NOVEMBER 1, 2014

Randy's earthly run was finished this morning at 9:05 a.m.

Overall it was a 42-hour waiting process to test, match, and find acceptable recipients. Both kidneys were placed, one to a female and another to a male. His liver was placed and his left lung. Tissue, eyes, bones, too! Heart was also accepted for a research hospital.

So Randy lives on!

His heavenly run has begun and we know he will do well.

We miss him terribly already but will continue to take this step-by-step. Please be patient as we make plans to celebrate this wonderful husband, father ... and much more. More to come!

Eleven

Thinking about all the families who benefited from my husband's organ donation was awesome to imagine.

Fargo's Sanford Hospital received letters from hospitals where the transplants were performed. Doctors reported that *all* of the transplants were successful, with recipients doing well.

I received a copy of the letter that was written by the organ transplant team to the doctors and caregivers back at the Fargo hospital. For some reason, I did not read it until four years later but it was such a powerful letter. It read:

Mr. B. had a donor designation and his family supported his decision to be a donor. He was able to give the gift of life to so many people. Below is the information we received from the transplant centers:

A 67-y.o. male who was COPD received a lung (the other was non-transplantable). The recipient is married with 2 children and was walking within 2 days post-op.

A 56-y.o. female received the liver. She is married and has 3 children and 5 grandchildren and loves to spend time with her family and watching grandkids, sports, and movies. What we learned from her transplant center was "she never thought she would receive a transplant."

A 54-y.o. male received a kidney. He is single and was doing well post-transplant.

A 51-y.o. male received the other kidney. He is married and is doing well.

His family authorized his heart to go to research, which will benefit many.

Twelve

The late afternoon drive back to Breckenridge was surreal.

We had spent much of the day at Steve and Darlene's house, surrounded by family and friends while we waited. Anxiousness seeped through me. I felt like I couldn't leave town until I knew that Randy's organs had been transferred to their recipients' hospitals and on to new life.

The hospital called about 3:00 p.m. All had gone well. It was finished. Organs, eyes, bones, and tissue were all on their way. Soon, his body would be transferred to the funeral home in Breckenridge. It was yet another painful step forward.

Although a sense of relief washed over me, my stomach stayed knotted, heavy, and hard, as I faced an unsettling future without Randy at my side.

Conversation, short and insignificant, kept the kids and me distracted on the short drive home. Lost in thought, I watched the clouds, wondering where Randy might be. But a block before our house, as the car turned onto Wegner Drive, the weight of my new reality slammed me. I was returning to *our* home, to *our* life, to *our* world.

Without Randy.

My knees turned to jelly when I stepped from the car and faced the short sidewalk leading to the front door. The same door Randy entered hundreds of times after his long day at work. When he would kick off his shoes and drop his over-stuffed backpack while Max jumped for joy and climbed all over him. Through that same door.

Never again.

It was just all too much to think about now. How could I enter the house where everything evoked memories of Randy and our life together? How could I face a future without him?

I was lost. Lost in front of my own house. I was alone. Alone while surrounded by loved ones.

This was *not* going to be easy.

I stiffened my knees, tried to steel my emotions, and forced myself forward. Emily came behind me and grabbed hold of me to stabilize my legs. We stopped for a long embrace, gathering enough strength to enter the house.

Reluctantly, I opened the door and paused in the entryway, half expecting to hear his voice or see his face.

What I encountered on the other side, amidst all the memories and painful reminders of Randy, were surprising little blessings. A crew of dear, thoughtful, empathetic friends had smoothed our way through what they knew would be a rough reentry. A bouquet of flowers on the dining room table. The fridge, freshly cleaned out, stuffed with our favorite comfort foods. An over-sized "care" basket—filled with special mementos that would help make our next few days a little more bearable. My people knew me well. They included a devotional book on grief, chocolates and other yummy treats, inspirational quotes, cards, and artifacts filled with encouraging Bible verses and advice on how to handle our grief. The basket brightened a corner of the dining room, waiting to ease us through the coming weeks.

My parents, sister Kathy, and her family joined us. I gathered my composure and settled for a while in the living room to visit.

"Excuse me," I said to no one in particular. "I think I'll go change into something more comfortable."

I made my way down the short hallway to our bedroom, now mine alone. I was unprepared for the shock that would shatter me when I flipped on the light. Alone, I stepped into the room and stopped in my tracks. There it was.

Our bed.

His dresser.

His wallet and watch sitting just as he had left it the night before he went for a run.

The scent of him still so strong on his clothes that I was overcome with hollowness.

His pillow smashed a bit as his head had left it.

Utter sadness possessed me as I set on the side of bed and cried. My heart was broken and my brain felt like mush.

How can this be my life? How can I go on without him?

A peculiar feeling reared its head, a feeling I hadn't felt since I was a kid away at Bible camp.

Homesickness!

I was homesick for Randy. Homesick for our life together. Homesick for the day-to-day normality I had so taken for granted.

I sighed and glanced again around the room, my eyes settling on a bouquet of fresh flowers on my nightstand. I reached for the note beside it.

All my love…always.
Love, Randy

It was from my friend Ann—who signed it from Randy. It

was as if God told her exactly what I would need in that moment as I faced home for the first time without Randy.

Deeply touched, I sat on the end of the bed and cried. Both sadness and comfort filled my heart. I knew without a doubt that we were loved. That we would be cared for. That people would come to our aid and see us through.

Thirteen

Planning and reminiscing, tears of sadness, and, yes, even tears of joy filled the following days. The kids and I had complete unity as we made preparations for our final sendoff for Randy. The wagons of family and friends circled tightly around us, and we were blessed by kindnesses during this time when our loss was still so fresh.

The cross-country team and some of the parents asked if they could come over one evening early in the week. I think they needed to be with us as much as we needed to be with them. We huddled around the bonfire telling heart-healing Coach Berndt stories and recalling the many special times they had as a team.

During this time, it became obvious that we needed to do a run in Randy's memory. We needed to take him off the side of the road and get him back to the school.

The team and I came up with the idea of a final "Run with Randy." Friends Janet and Ann already had the wheels in motion, with tee-shirt orders pending. Micayla and Jared, a niece and nephew, created a design and Run with Randy (RWR) logo print-ready. We were well on our way.

The team jumped in and took care of race details. It made the most sense to have the event kick off the memorial services, so we settled on a Wednesday 8:06 a.m. run, corresponding to the final stride Randy had taken just days prior.

Much like everything else planned for Randy, crowds and TV cameras showed up. November 6th was a bitterly cold day with a light mist and snow in the air, but the team, family, friends, and community members ran their hearts out for Coach Berndt.

We finished the run. We finished *his* run.

• • • • • • • •

During preparations for Randy's funeral, a looming logistical element haunted me: Where to hold the service? Our strong affiliation with the United Methodist Church had me torn: Should we have his funeral service in the sanctuary there? Or should we consider the size of the crowd that might attend to honor my husband and find a place to seat that many?

When Randy's good friend and former pastor of our church, Pastor Terry, arrived, I asked if he would lead the service and he graciously accepted. He voiced concerns that echoed my internal turmoil.

"Jana, I really think the church won't hold all the people who will want to attend," he said.

Diane, superintendent of Breckenridge Schools and a close friend, made my decision easy by offering the use of school facilities. When I agreed, she blessed us by arranging the use of the middle school gymnasium where Randy had taught, coached, and touched the lives of hundreds of community members.

Her resources transformed the gym into a beautifully personal sanctuary. Religious cross and all!

The evening of Randy's visitation and prayer service, a long line of community members serpentined outside the building, through the door, and down the hallway—all waiting patiently to pay their respects. They filed by a loving display of photographs and artifacts depicting the too-short life of my fifty-two-year-old husband. The kids and I were well loved, comforted with generous hugs, individual prayers, and a slew of stories from the steady stream of well-wishers—some were dear friends, others strangers.

The emotional four hours of conversing, responding, ushering people toward my husband's casket. Of accepting condolences. Of comforting the comforters in their own grief. Of standing through it all ….

The evening drained me. Physically and emotionally. The mental toll left me empty.

The kind of empty that couldn't be filled by food or water. It was the kind of empty that required quiet—quiet time at home.

As I drove back to the house, my thoughts turned toward the following day, one more day of saying our goodbyes. The vision of the funeral played through my mind.

God, please let this be what Randy would have wanted.

I thought about pallbearers and supposed we might ask his brothers—Gary, Steven, and Keith—along with his sister Amy, Jim (my sister Kathy's husband), and longtime friends, John, Kent, Mark, and Dennis. These were the people who carried Randy throughout his life on earth; it seemed fitting they would carry his casket as a sort of escort to heaven.

My kids and I hoped to honor their dad by including his favorite scriptures as a way of sharing the faith and hope by which he lived his life. We also gave much thought and consideration to the most appropriate music for the service.

"Blessings," a song written by Laura Story, had been a family favorite that year, but its message held a newly significant meaning as we planned Randy's funeral. He had especially loved listening to Emily sing it in the living room, or at church, with me accompanying at the piano.

Worried whether or not we would have the courage and strength to get through the song, Emily and I decided we could do it for Randy. But we feared it wouldn't sound the same on a borrowed keyboard. To be the way Randy loved it most, it needed to be played on a piano. Not just any piano, but my piano from home.

"Do you suppose …" Emily hesitated to finish her thought, but I had had the same idea.

Knowing full well how far-fetched the idea really was and that, on any normal day, our request might be ridiculous, we plunged ahead and contacted the store where I originally purchased the piano and asked for input.

"Steve," they suggested. "He's a piano mover who will do the job for you."

It turned out we didn't need to worry about sounding crazy because with this idea came another blessing. Steve, a recent widower, had a special compassion in his heart for us and understood our need to honor Randy with this song.

Fourteen

On the day of the funeral, the crowded gymnasium cradled his casket. I was amazed and humbled that more than a thousand friends gathered to honor my husband with kind words and deeds. My prized piano stood in place, ready for me to play as Emily sang her heart out for her dad, just as she had done many times before.

I couldn't believe Emily and I were able to make it through the song. To do the impossible in the midst of our sadness. We were told afterward that our moving performance and message of hope brought a thousand people to their feet in a standing ovation. For both Emily and I this was our final act of service for Randy, a moment to treasure.

Following the funeral, we gathered with close friends and family at The Wilkin, a local restaurant Randy favored. Kayla, the server he liked best, was assigned to our table and was especially attentive to our needs throughout the evening. The wagon had circled and circled again, many times throughout the week.

We had celebrated Randy's life, said our farewells, shared a meal. *It's over,* I thought as I looked around the room at the dear faces of those closest to us, desperately missing the dearest one of all.

These loved ones had been with us since Randy fell; now they needed to return to their routines, to catch up on what they had missed after gathering and rallying around us, sacrificing nearly two weeks of their lives for us.

After a deep breath to take it all in, I knew I had to step into the future without Randy.

As our beloved friends and family left us that night, we kissed and hugged and promised to stay in touch. The sendoff was deeply emotional. But as sad and scared as we were, there was also a sense of readiness on our part. As a family, we knew we had to move forward. We needed to discover what life was going to look and feel like.

Would we sink or would we swim? Now we would start navigating life without Randy. It was time to discover, bit by bit, our new norm.

As hard as it was, I sensed in my heart God telling me: *You have to take this next step, but I've got you. Trust Me.*

Fifteen

As each felt ready in his own time, the boys stepped into their new normal, as well. Tyler returned to Minneapolis and resumed his career. Emily's fiancé, Mitchell, headed back to college in Nashville. Matthew, of course, was still living at home. Emily chose to stay longer with me.

The week following the funeral, Emily, Matthew and I flew to Nashville to meet with her professors to see what her options would be at college. She wanted to finish the semester from home while staying on track to graduate in the spring. Thankfully, professors at Belmont University were accommodating and sympathetic to her situation.

While we were in Nashville, Emily needed to present a speech as one of her finals. She rewrote her planned presentation and, instead, spoke about organ donation. I sat in the back of the room with Mitchell and Matthew, listening to my girl tell about her dad and his death and the life-giving gift he gave to so many through organ donation. Her delivery was real and she expressed deep feelings and thoughts. I don't know how Emily did it, but she did, with grace and grief only a loving daughter could muster. I don't know how we listened, but we did, with emotions still raw and tender.

I felt sympathy and sorrow sweep through the classroom as students watched my twenty-one-year-old from Minnesota deliver the speech of her life.

It was no surprise to any of us that her speech earned an "A." Given the subject and personal details shared, it was quite remarkable.

We flew home after the long weekend. Matthew returned to high school on Monday, and I began thinking about my job and how I would handle my own return.

I worked for a banking organization at the time of Randy's death and had been with the company for almost thirty years. Understanding and supportive, my boss was patient and helpful as I tentatively eased back into the corporate world. I had always believed that I worked for a great organization, but this proved again the awesomeness of my team.

Going back to work was a huge hurdle, one I had to take at my own pace. I had reservations. I dreaded the intimate questions, the compassionate comments and condolences … even hugs of comfort. I would relive the pain of Randy's absence a little bit with each kind gesture.

My first day back, I found it difficult and draining to talk to coworkers and clients. At this place where I once wore the hat of confident "boss," I returned a different person. An uncertain, inexperienced widow. So much had changed. So much had happened.

My work life and my personal life, two separate worlds but now I had to start to figure how to navigate them in my new role. For the last few weeks, the two had collided and now I needed to separate them. I learned to navigate through this rather quickly.

The best way to keep my composure while at work was to not offer more detail than was asked.

"How are you doing?" was a typical opening question.

"I'm doing well, considering the last few weeks." My simple, reassuring response seemed to end the conversation.

But I imagined it was difficult from the perspective of coworkers and clients, too. I pictured them thinking, *What do I say to her? If I don't ask, will she think I don't care? If I do bring it up, will I make her cry? It's so obvious, but how do I tell her I care without making her feel bad?*

I wanted them to say *something* to acknowledge my situation. But I preferred it be simple, short, and sweet. Perhaps something that didn't require more than a thank you from me. Something like, "I'm so sorry for your loss. I've been thinking about you."

Stepping outside of my grief to rejoin the workforce was a sobering reminder that the world-at-large was still spinning—even though my own had collapsed around me.

Life, I was learning, goes on with you or without you.

Year One

OVERCOMING HOMESICKNESS

· ·

Sixteen

Why can't time simply stop? I wondered. *Just for a little while.*

The days were sprinting by too fast and I couldn't keep up with them. Didn't want to keep up with them. It was as if everyone else was driving the speed limit and I was stuck at the stop sign. I wanted to sit still and wait. Wait for the light to change. Wait for the Lord to remove my pain so I could go on.

The simple task of picking up some groceries became a massive undertaking. Seeing the world moving on in spite of our upside down life was so evident in a grocery store. Small talk with familiar faces and a few hugs from closer acquaintances gave me a sneak peek of how the next weeks and months might look and feel. Everything, everyone around me was continuing on like normal, but I was moving in slow motion.

Three weeks prior to Randy's passing, we dealt with the untimely death of his father. Randy's mother had died when he was about ten, and now he found himself facing life without his father. It was a tough loss, but he, his stepmom, and siblings were dealing with it together. Randy was a strong man of God and had an amazing faith to help carry him through the loss.

One day while perusing Facebook, I stumbled upon a post from Randy, written shortly after his dad's funeral. I found it oddly comforting to read how similar his feelings were to what I found myself experiencing.

Randy Berndt
October 14, 2014 · Breckenridge ·

Its been a little over a week now since our family laid our wonderful father,grandfather,husband, and father-in-law to rest. Struggling to get back into the swing of things, a good friend of ours perhaps said it best;" for the week or so at the end, your families' worlds stopped. Time, and the rest of the world kept going, and that is difficult to reconcile ." As we play catch up, we are so thankful for all the expressions of sympathy and support we have received from so many extended family members and friends - a simple "Thank You" seems so inadequate,but know that our thanks comes from the heart. Life does go on, as it should. With the help of our loving families and friends, and most importantly, with a loving God, we too will go on, grateful we had the chance to have our dad in our lives, and secure in the knowledge that he is with his Lord. Thanks again to all.

You, Kathy Sipe Lesnar, Jim Lesnar and 51 others   6 Comments 6 Shares

👍 Like   💬 Comment

Seventeen

In the months that followed, it became increasing difficult
to verbalize my grief and feelings, to express where I was in the
mourning process. Because my emotions were so unpredictable,
I found it too risky to be open about my mourning, fearing a
complete meltdown.

Publicly, I put on a happy face and changed the subject
as quickly as possible. The same question and concern for my
wellbeing became a daily conversation starter by almost everyone
I encountered. How my heart wanted to respond and how my brain
told me to answer were quite different. The shorter the response,
the quicker I could return a question to change the subject. These
awkward moments continued for weeks (even months) after
Randy's death.

How often have I been guilty of the same offense? I
reflected. *How often have I asked someone how they were doing?*
Such a normal and innocent inquiry. Yet, for a widow or someone

experiencing loss, the painful question was loaded. You fight the impulse to answer with something like:

"Really? Do you want the honest truth? My heart is broken and I'm sad and I absolutely don't want to do life without my husband."

A response like that might set someone back in their tracks, so instead you end up telling a little white lie: "I'm doing as well as I can."

Instead, I decided, going forward I would exchange the question I once posed to grieving friends for a more thoughtful, encouraging comment:

"It's good to see you," I would say with warmth and sincerity. "I've been thinking of and praying for you."

On the other hand, at home with family and close friends I took a measure of comfort in talking about Randy. As time moved along, so did the conversations about our mutual loved one. I found a sense of safety within a circle of close friends who shared love and friendship with my husband. We talked and laughed often about him—how he insisted on researching every household purchase by reading *Consumer Reports*, or how he always managed to be in the bathroom the minute we were ready to say the dinner prayer. "Randy Stories" we called them. Although often poignant, those shared memories—funny, truthful, and touching—warmed my heart and soothed the healing process.

Near the six-month anniversary of his death, an internal conflict began brewing a bit of a storm in my belly. Even though I had grown stronger, a mental switch flipped when it felt like society expected me to stop talking about my husband. Conversations became even more uneasy and awkward. I didn't know whether I should talk about Randy and those I conversed with didn't know either.

I imagined them wondering: "Should we bring up Randy's name? Or would that be inappropriate? Will it just make her sad?"

I began worrying, *Should I say Randy's name out loud or*

will that make this person feel uneasy?

Oh, how this grieving widow hoped people would talk about my Randy. "Yes!" I longed to say. "Please include Randy in our visits. No, it's not inappropriate. And no, talking about him does not make me sad."

What saddened me was *not* remembering him, not interjecting his name, the thought that others would forget him.

Like he was gone ... and had never existed.

Eighteen

During the deepest, darkest days as I cried myself to sleep each night, I found solace in my religion, in my faith and in my favorite scriptures.

I was never more grateful for being raised in a family that knew Jesus and taught me about Him. I was never more grateful for a husband who knew Jesus and lived out his faith every single day for his family and the world to see.

As broken as I was, I wondered, *Where would I be in my grief if I didn't have Jesus and the hope of His promise of eternal life?* His sustaining strength and courage, along with the support of family and friends, has and continues to be my saving grace.

Many times when our family faced a difficult time or life handed us more than we thought we could handle, Randy would reach for his brown leather Bible and read this to us:

*I lift my eyes to the hills—where does my help come from?
My help comes from the Lord, the Maker of heaven and earth.
He will not let your foot slip— He who watches over you will
not slumber; the Lord will keep you from all harm— He will watch
over your life; the Lord will watch over your coming and going both
now and forevermore.* (Psalm 121:1-4,7,8 NIV)

After Randy's death, the kids and I often found comfort
in this verse as we faced the huge mountain we had to climb. I
repeated these reassuring words on the nights I couldn't sleep and
was challenged to trust a little deeper.

Now, I reached for my own Bible and read an equally
familiar scripture that teaches us to give thanks in all things.

"It doesn't say 'give thanks for *all* circumstances,'" I
muttered, "but to give thanks *no matter what* circumstances you find
yourself facing."

It was my duty to find something to be grateful for, no
matter what I was going through.

Gratitude.

I'm a firm believer that no matter where I find myself at in
my own journey, God sees me and knows where I am. He has me
right where He wants me and if He wants me somewhere different, I
can trust Him to make it happen.

I couldn't give thanks that my husband died; my kids
certainly weren't grateful that their dad was no longer present. But
I knew I needed to trust Him and to look for something, anything to
be thankful for even as I dealt with this massive loss.

And so, I reinstituted my personal, powerful practice of
gratitude–in the midst of unspeakable heartache.

*I can be grateful for the twenty-eight years that I was
married to an incredible man.*

I can be grateful for the blessing of our wonderful children.

*I can be grateful for years of memories—and the thousands
of pictures documenting them.*

In lonely moments of stillness, I added to my growing list of blessings, recalling simple gestures that went a long way to heal us and carry us through our quiet season of grief.

The Sunday after Randy's passing, Beth arrived with her "beauty kit." My long-time hair stylist and classmate of Randy's, she tenderly took care of me, my hair, and my spirit. Who knew that your hair stylist made house calls? Not only did she help me, she ended up doing my mom's hair and my sister's, too. We all gathered around that small kitchen table to trade more Randy stories while readying ourselves for the upcoming services of remembrance.

The healing and conversation that took place in those couple of hours was so good for all of us. Beth's kindness, her gentleness in that moment was love-in-action, love as a verb.

Each week for one full year, I received a card and short message from my sister-in-law Barb. Some humorous, others with a scrawled short message about her family. She stayed connected to me and nourished my soul. She showed love through her actions.

Diane, Ann, and several other friends checked in often through texting. Nothing big or deep, just a simple line or two. "Hey, thinking of you today and praying your day goes well!" went a long way toward making me feel loved.

My friend Marcia arranged to meet me often at the nutrition club over protein shakes to simply listen to whatever was on my mind. On those days, I especially appreciated her background in social work.

Friends Kent and Annette met us often for meals at the Wilkin Eatery, my husband's favorite restaurant, to check up and see how we were doing. Our longtime friendship paved the way to talk about Randy and how much we missed him.

Our go-to family, The Richmans, adopted us as their own. Marcia with her thoughtful advice, John assisting Matthew with my honey-do projects, dinners with all of us, season tickets to Bison college basketball games … the list goes on and on. Their friendship was (and continues to be) a strong part of who we are today.

Another blessing I appreciated was a fortuitous timing of events that allowed us to purchase a cabin on a lake with my sister's family and our parents. A cabin on a lake had always been Randy's dream for us, and though he might not have pictured it exactly like this, it was comforting to know we were making his hope a reality.

Buck Saw Lodge—our lake home—was officially established in June of 2015, a positive steppingstone. Nothing heals the heart more than peaceful pontoon rides, a brisk walk around the lake, and delicious family meals accompanied by stories, laughter … and tears.

Honestly I'm not sure if the kids or I truly realized the magnitude of kindnesses we received. The days, weeks, and months were filled with people doing what they could to help us survive our tragedy. Although I knew I couldn't recall and note each deed, I was grateful to be so well loved by so many.

Nineteen

My early morning routine became a special time for me in the following months. Even before getting out of bed—or scrolling through social media—I spent some quiet time with God.

Jesus Calling, by Sarah Young, became my daily devotional book. I felt that God spoke to me through the author's words. One lesson was profound: *Think of your life as an adventure, with Me as your Guide and Companion. Don't worry about where our path will lead tomorrow—just live in the adventure of today. Keep your mind on staying close to Me."*

I had to remind myself multiple times a day, *Don't get ahead of yourself.* Easier said than done, of course, but it was a practice I vowed to keep learning.

Anyone who knows me at all knows that step-by-step and one-day-at-a-time is not my normal M.O. Widowhood, in many ways, forced a sort of personality change in me. I had to learn to slow down, pause, take a breath, and remind myself, *Stop worrying*

about tomorrow. It's not here yet!
    Patience is a virtue.

That common phrase rang throughout my childhood and well into my adult life. I could still hear my mother reciting it over and over during the moments when I was impatient and wanted my peanut butter sandwich NOW!

"Patience is a virtue."

This was a virtue I needed to develop after so great a loss. It was a season to be kind to myself. To give myself grace and time to work through my grief. As unnerving as it was to believe, I knew my heart would heal in time. It would heal in *my* time. It would heal in God's time.

How wonderful if learning patience was all there was to grief. But as soon as I was getting the hang of that virtue, a new issue derailed me.

Twenty

Worry.

There were many moments when crushing grief and
heartbreak ravaged my heart and mind. This happened most often
when I feared a future without Randy.

My worry was real, as it is for most widows. It consumed
my thoughts. It paralyzed me to the point that even simple decisions
became insurmountable.

When our annual tax appointment arrived, I struggled
to concentrate, to gather receipts, bank statements, and other tax
records for my longtime friend and preparer Jim.

*So simple, Jana. You've done this for years. Why is it
suddenly difficult?*

Was it a focus issue? A denial issue? Or was my mind so
consumed with the haves and have-nots of unwelcome singledom?

I needed Randy!

I pawed frantically through stacks of papers, a forceful

wave of stress pushing against my chest.

What if I miss something vital? What if I owe a bunch of money to the IRS? What about ....

Stop it, Jana, I ordered. *Just stop. Calm down. You're getting ahead of yourself.*

In these moments of panic and anxiety, I forced my mind to the here and now. The next breath. The next minute. The next hour. If I could stay present, the next step seemed more manageable.

The knot of worry, which made my stomach clench, was usually a red flag warning: *You're getting ahead of yourself.* I had taken too many steps, moved too fast. I was learning that there was a delicate balance between grieving in the present and dwelling on troubling thoughts about what might—or might not—yet happen.

Balancing the two was, of course, the answer to my problem.

I remembered watching my babies when they learned to be independent. They learned to creep before they learned to crawl and to crawl before they learned to toddle and to toddle before they learned to walk. Before I knew it, they were running around the house.

But they took a lot of spills before they learned to run.

Grief was similar, I decided. You had to take many baby steps—that sometimes felt like you were literally crawling out of the valley of death—before you could walk. Eventually, you would learn to walk again, and one day you would find yourself in a new normal, running through life like you once did. Almost.

On days that seemed too much to bear, I recognized I was most worried about a future with the kids moving on, leaving me behind. In the house. Alone. The angst of widowhood knotted with the apprehension of an empty nest until I couldn't distinguish between my thoughts and feelings.

On long evening walks, Randy and I had dreamed about our future. Travel plans, retirement goals, all exciting and enticing. But even on those strolls around the neighborhood, I would confess to struggling with thoughts of an empty nest in my near future. What would I do once I wasn't a mom anymore?

"Mom-hood doesn't expire," Randy reminded me. "That's a title that will always hold steadfast."

What the kids would require would simply be different. While I might not need to cook, clean, and care for their everyday health and basic needs, they would need me so much more emotionally. He reassured me often that it would all be good; we'd have each other and, oh, how exciting that would be.

A popular song—Matt Maher's "Lord, I Need You"—rose to the top of my playlist at the time of Randy's heart attack. Emily played it on her phone repeatedly as we sat at his bedside.

> *Lord, I need you. Oh, I need you.*
> *Every hour I need you.*
> *My one defense, my righteousness,*
> *Oh God how I need you!*

After listening multiple times, the lyrics began to fully sink in when I was drowning in *what ifs*, feeling completely hopeless and helpless in the situation. The message ministered to my heart in those moments when I didn't know what to do and needed the Lord to give me peace. As a family, we needed Him to take away the worry and uncertainty of our future.

Months afterward, it was one of my go-to anthems when my thoughts ran too far ahead and worry overtook me.

I couldn't do this alone. I just couldn't. I needed God's love. I needed my support team. And I needed to let go, fully accepting that I was not in control.

What I needed more than anything was to understand, "You are God. I am not."

God was leading me every step of the way and He hadn't and wouldn't lead me astray.

My constant prayer became, "Lord, please help me. Help

me stay right here, right now, and carry me through this day. Protect me, Lord, from worry and guide me in Your care."

I asked the Lord to protect my heart and mind and keep me in His perfect peace. I desired a release from the panic and anxiety of thinking about how I might live through and navigate the rest of my life.

The future was yet to come. I would stay present.

Twenty-one

I struggled to keep my head on straight in the weeks that followed. Regular life events, piled on top of the trauma of losing a loved one while *trying* to give myself space and time to grieve was nearly driving me over the edge. I kept my eyes on God, knowing only He could get me through. But my children had journeys of their own to navigate.

One evening while sleeping upstairs, in a room I was slowly starting to call my own, I had a vivid, comforting dream of Randy visiting me in our new home. (During this same time, I was debating whether to buy the lake cabin with my sister and parents.) The dream was different than anything I had ever experienced: startlingly realistic and memorable.

When I awoke in the morning, I vividly recalled minute details of the encounter: what Randy said, what he wore, and how he looked. A new sense of peace settled over me, as soothing and comforting as a favorite blanket.

It was as if Randy had said, "You're fine, Jana, and I'm here for you."

Soon after, I phoned my brother-in law Jim. "Let's do it! Let's buy the lake place."

Most books about grieving and most grief counseling materials advise those who experience significant loss to not make big changes during the first year. In fact, they emphasize steering clear of major decision-making during that time frame. The advice is sound.

My ability to make decisions and feel comfortable with change was rocky. My frame of mind and confidence were shaky. Unfortunately for us, so much happened outside of our control.

In the immediate aftermath of Randy's death, we needed to celebrate Matthew's eighteenth birthday, the big birthday that exultantly shouts: "Look at me! I'm officially a grownup! I am an adult! " No kid should have to celebrate this milestone immediately after losing his dad.

But celebrate we did, and we did it right.

Always a car buff, Matthew knows most makes, models, and details of practically every automobile that rolls off the assembly line. As a young boy, he lined the house with his collection of hundreds of Matchbox-type vehicles.

Fittingly, my sister's family rented a Hummer limousine on the night of his birthday. Outfitted with choice snacks and beverages and with current top hits pounding from the speakers, the limo carted us all to Fargo for dinner at his favorite steakhouse. The evening rounded off with dessert at Cherry Berry, the yogurt shop he adored.

Surprisingly, the party was a nice distraction from our fresh sorrow, a soothing balm for our bruised spirits.

Because he would be graduating from high school the following spring, Matthew had big decisions to make involving his future and college. Naturally, confronting those choices without his dad's input was emotional and painful.

Twenty-two

November was birthday month at the Sipe-Berndt household. My son Matthew's was followed by mine. Being the third Sipe sibling to celebrate a November birthday, mere weeks before Christmas, I especially loved my birthday. Picking out my favorite meal and sharing my gift list with loved ones ... sitting at the table while others waited on me, doing dishes, and cleaning up after the party.

Memories of an earlier birthday, when Randy took the day off from work and prepared my favorite meal, swept over me. His homemade meatballs, freshly peeled and mashed potatoes, creamed baby carrots and milk-sausage gravy filled many pots and pans. He was so proud of his hours of labor ... well, with maybe a little guidance from his mother-in-law whom he consulted on the sly. It stood out as special largely because of the love Randy showed with his junior chef skills. Upping his typical boxed macaroni to a homemade meatball dinner was love-in-action. In colossal form.

It felt selfish on my part, but Randy was a big reason why my birthday was always special. His studious selection of birthday cards, yes, I mean *cards* was extensive. Three minimum. He simply couldn't home in on only one for his special wife; it took several to get the message across.

My first birthday without Randy happened to fall on Thanksgiving, which seemed especially fitting. A day to be thankful for family, friends, and the rich blessings in my life. Praying as a family over our meal, we thanked God for our time with Randy, a painful reminder that his chair sat empty.

Leftovers were more abundant that holiday. Maybe because Randy wasn't there to eat his fair share. Or maybe the rest of us didn't have the appetite typically aroused for this much-anticipated holiday at the Sipe family house.

As November seeped into December, I faced the daunting task of tackling Christmas traditions from our childhoods along with the many we added as a Berndt family.

Decorations, caroling with friends, the annual Community Christmas Choir Cantata, fondue on Christmas Eve … I could picture Randy's long fork hanging in the fondue pot until every last drop of Swiss cheese was gone. There were gifts to plan and purchase and wrap and tie with ribbon. There were cards to write, cookies to bake … traditions that added up to stress. It wasn't by chance that the Berndt favorite seasonal movie was National Lampoon's "Christmas Vacation." Our house and traditions stacked right up there with Clark Griswold's.

I tackled the tree one quiet Sunday afternoon. Unwrapping family heirlooms and ornaments was a walk down memory lane, always a beloved experience for Randy, the kids, and me. Amy Grant crooned "I'll be Home for Christmas" through the Bluetooth speaker.

That did it. That was all I could take of tree decorating.

Emily, busy with homework at the kitchen table, felt my distress and joined me. Together we cried our way through the remaining box of ornaments.

Midstream in the decorating, we stepped back to admire our labor of love.

She crinkled her nose. "Do you smell that, Mom?"

I sniffed the air. "Yes, almost smells like something burning." I scanned the room. "What it is? Where is it coming from?"

In no time, we noticed a flash in the center of the artificial tree. The extension cord we had used for years threw a spark and was seconds from igniting a fire. Emily, swifter than me, grabbed the plug and yanked it from the wall. The thought of what could have been sent chills down my spine.

Yet I couldn't help but wonder, *Was it Randy sending us a little love? Telling us, 'I'm here with you girls. I know this one is tough, but I'm here with you.'* The thought warmed me.

• • • • • • • •

Music during the Christmas season has been central to our tradition, whether carols on the radio or participating in musical events as a family. For many years, we had participated in the Community Christmas Choir Cantata. With me at the piano, Emily and her dad passionately sang the message of hope and love.

Rehearsals began before Randy's heart attack, so he had been attending with the choral group to the extent that he had hand-written notes in his copy of "Silent Night, Holy Night." I missed a number of rehearsals after his collapse and eventual death, but good friend Joyce stepped in and rehearsed with the choir for many weeks in my stead.

The night of the first performance, I started playing, "Jesus, the Center of It All." The thirty-piece orchestra joined in, then the conductor, Kent, cued in the choir. Several measures into the choral part, emotion overcame me. The song's words were so powerful I was unable to read the notes on the blurred page before me.

Joyce, on standby in the middle row of the riser, would have come to my rescue, but before that could happen Emily saw my face and acted quickly. She ducked behind the bleacher and scooted next to me on the piano bench, calming me enough with her comfort and strength to make it through the song.

Much of the yuletide season remained hazy, never even registering in my memory. But December 24 and 25 were spent quite differently than ever before. They remain unforgettable.

● ● ● ● ● ● ●

We spent our first Christmas without Randy in Florida with my extended Sipe family. My sister, Kathy, and her family; my brother, Mike, and his family; and my parents gathered at their southern Florida condo. The kids and I nested at the home of the Rasmussens, Minnesota friends of my folks who kindly offered their place for the week. It was just what we needed. Their three-bedroom bungalow allowed the kids and I to share a quiet, private space. Poised in the living room was an enticing grand piano, healing therapy for my weeping heart.

This was the first time the kids and I had ever spent the holidays away from home, probably the best thing for us to do at that time. Fully understanding and expecting difficulty no matter where we observed Christmas, we made it a point to remember and honor Randy. Despite hard moments, we made the most of our time together.

I viewed the traditional Christmas Eve church service though a new lens as I envisioned Randy in heaven, with Baby Jesus on His birthday.

Balmy, warm morning walks encouraged intimate conversations and free-flowing tears to carry us through the week.

Even in Florida, we managed to uphold our life-long fondue tradition, but it tasted flat. There were extra helpings of cheese left in the bottom of the pot.

• • • • • • • •

Immediately after the Christmas rush, a reluctant Emily needed to return to college. On track for a spring graduation, she faced the challenge of a tough semester ahead, compounded by her deep grief and the difficulty of leaving her brother and me at home to sludge through life-without-Randy. In January, we traveled to Nashville to get her settled, both of us wary about the distance and separation.

My own hesitation grew into that odd sense of homesickness. This time for my daughter and our time together.

While our minds told us we would be only a phone call or FaceTime away, our hearts ached with the anticipation of separation. Now closer than ever, Emily and I had not been apart since Randy's death.

I sorted my scrambled thoughts, looking for a balm to soothe the angst we both felt. Something, anything to make our time apart bearable.

"Let's make a plan," I suggested. "For when we can get together next."

Emily's brow wrinkled in thought. "Well, we get a long weekend over President's Day."

That was it! A long weekend to regroup. We would find a way to be together in a just a few weeks.

A small voice chanted in my head, *You can do this, Jana, you can do this.*

Twenty-three

February and March brought the painful process of touching and packing every single item in our house on Maple Street.

Three weeks prior to Randy's death, we had purchased a new home several blocks away. Because the seller was building a house, it would be March before we were able to take possession. And now March was upon me.

I couldn't imagine having to handle a move like this by myself. It was a blessing that I had the extra few months to grieve in our home before moving. Then in March, with family and friends right by our side, we moved—into the home of Randy's and my dreams.

Much like our year thus far, we had our inner circle of family, friends, and neighbors to bolster us.

Several weeks earlier, Matthew, Steven and Kathy's husband Jim, two of Randy's close friends, John and Kent, as well as Mitchell, packed up the garage and shed. Randy's domain. His man cave.

Tools, golf clubs, running gear … along with plenty of junk that should have been discarded years ago. Mounted on the back wall was his prizcd possession: new, used-only-once, Fisher downhill skis. Randy had saved for months and researched even longer for the perfect pair.

The garage project hinted at how it would feel and look to sort through the other items in our house. Touching, smelling, evaluating every item Randy ever owned, an intimidating nightmare for sure.

I found myself peering into the trailer, surveying all of Randy's worldly possessions and wondering.

Can I really go through with this move?

Can I possibly leave all the memories assembled in this house?

The last house, the last home where my husband lived.

My realtor's husband, Charlie, loaned his construction trailer to store the garage items until we moved later in the month. The fellows filled it to the brim. They also crammed the dumpster to capacity.

Upon our return from a morning bridal shower for Emily, I greeted the crew of diligent workers. Their weary eyes and dragging bodies revealed the emotional strain of the arduous purging process. Fortunately, they did it all without requiring anything of me. I didn't need to look over, handle, or make decisions on a single item.

The remainder of the month, every spare moment was consumed with culling, choosing, and packing everything that would make its way to Crescent Drive. Most widows might not deal with their loved one's personal possessions until after the first year, but the move necessitated some uncomfortable choices. The local dumpsite probably groaned at the weight of discards from one household. And I could not believe how much *stuff* a math teacher needed to save and store to do his job. *Really, Randy?*

For more than a quarter of a century, we had lived and

loved. We knew pretty much everything about each other. But the feeling of going through Randy's most treasured items was no elementary task. We had built our marriage on trust, with no reason to question it, but handling his possessions felt like an invasion of his personal space. A violation of that sacred trust.

What if I find something he didn't want me to see? What if he had secrets?

Jana, I scolded, *you have no basis for these irrational thoughts. This is just crazy.*

These are the things I encountered: His wallet with credit cards and old crinkled receipts. Family photos, torn and tattered from years of carrying them. His Bible with notes scribbled in the margins, old church bulletins bookmarking the pages he frequented.

His dress slacks and jeans, socks, pajamas. His shirts. A favorite button-down shirt he wore to school most Fridays. A golf polo from the Pebble Beach course, the trip we made for our fifteenth wedding anniversary.

Randy's golf shirts still had the strong smell of his aftershave. I held them close, sniffed, found myself caught up in the alarming yet comforting aroma of him. I clung to a few of my favorites—and made a quiet decision to not pack or give away everything.

An amazing thing happened while rummaging through my husband's things. I had an epiphany: It was all just "stuff." Stuff Randy didn't take with him. Stuff that had no value to him after death. So, why was I making it seem more important than it was?

Memories were mine to cherish regardless of how much paraphernalia I held onto.

Suddenly, the process lightened, became easier. I gave myself permission to release this attachment to items that would wither and fade with time and, instead, held the memories close, knowing they would grow ever more special with time.

Even so—on those days when my emotions weighed extra heavily—I found myself reaching into a cubby in the armoire for solace.

His scent was still so real. How could it be that he was gone?

• • • • • • • •

The Monday before Easter, with Kathy and Emily at my side, I closed on the house purchase, signing my life away to move into another phase of widowhood. Family, friends, and new neighbors jumped in to help and the move went off without a hitch. Within several days we were settled into our new home.

And then came "The Extreme Make-over on Crescent Drive," as one neighbor affectionately called it.

Emily and Mitchell made the trek back from Nashville to join Kathy's family, who came for the week, and my parents who flew in from Florida. My brother Todd and his wife joined us as we burned the midnight candle for a solid week, stripping wallpaper and rolling on fresh paint. While contractors re-shingled the roof, John and Mathew handled some light carpentry; Kent and his brother Paul installed updated lighting throughout, Mark laid flooring, and Dick painted bedrooms until he couldn't see straight.

The wish list Randy and I had made for "someday" turned into a week of as-long-as-you-have-all-this-help-you-might-as-well-just do-it-now.

Steve, the piano mover, arrived to do his part again and gently placed my beloved grand piano into the freshly redecorated living room. Randy would have been so pleased.

Family and friends turned the new house into *our* new home. We turned the page to a new chapter in the Berndt family.

Twenty-four

The next few weeks were a flurry of activity, stepping up the momentum right into a busy spring. I chaperoned Matthew's senior band trip—which happened to be to Nashville. Twenty hours on a school bus with ninety exuberant teenagers and their parent chaperones afforded me a memory I may want to erase but also an opportunity to check on Emily. We arrived home just in time to head back to Nashville for Emily's—and her fiancé Mitchell's—college graduations from Belmont University. Their ceremonies were split, Emily's in the morning followed by Mitchell's after lunch. This gave us the opportunity to meet Mitchell's family, who arrived from Pennsylvania.

Emily's graduation was a breaking point of grief with all that these past five months had handed her. Mitchell, Matthew, and I were in the stadium seats at the Belmont Curb Event Center patiently waiting for Emily's turn to walk across the stage when Mitchell had a suspicious feeling that something was seriously wrong with her.

He darted through the arena and worked his way backstage until he found Emily, curled in a ball, frozen in her grief, nowhere near ready or able to receive her diploma. A few hours earlier, she had donned her Run with Randy tee-shirt under her graduation robe and strapped on her fluorescent pink Run with Randy running shoes, ready to do this. Now, struck with a panic attack, she felt paralyzed.

How could she walk across the stage without her dad in the stadium?

From the day Emily first shared her dream of going to college in Nashville, it was her dad who had encouraged, prompted, and pushed her to this point. Now he wasn't here to see her achieve her dream.

Mitchell talked sweetly, yet persuasively to Emily and helped her regain enough composure to take the long, dutiful walk across the Belmont University graduation stage.

With my eyes wet and my heart pounding in my chest, I ached for my daughter.

How unfair this life is. I'm so sorry for my little girl. Her dad would be so proud.

Twenty-five

Two short weeks after graduation, we faced a significant family event: Emily's and Mitchell's wedding. There are many normal emotions that surround the milestone of marriage, but with loss so fresh in our hearts, the joyous event cast a harrowing shadow.

Saddened that Randy wouldn't be there in the ways we had envisioned, we somehow managed to throw ourselves into wedding plans—an unexpected blessing that forced us to look forward rather than get too stuck in the past.

Ironically, wedding talk started in September of 2013 when we got the call from Emily that she had a new "friend"—who turned into a very *good* friend. It wasn't long before my mother's intuition kicked in; I knew this friend meant so much more. Emily, I could tell, was in love.

When December arrived, Emily came home for holiday break and walked around like a lost puppy missing her best friend. Randy and I made a surprise decision to fly Mitchell out to Minnesota for New Year's weekend. We justified that it would be a good chance to meet this young man who had stolen our daughter's heart. In hindsight, God had a bigger plan: Mitchell needed to "meet the parents" and start making memories.

Randy and I arranged to pick him up midweek at the nearby airport, with the day's high temperature forecast at a balmy -25 degrees Fahrenheit and wind chill temps of -45 degrees. Even for lifelong Minnesotans, those were bitter numbers.

Mitchell would later tell how his mother in Pennsylvania heard about our frigid weather and had said to him, "I can't imagine what that cold air would feel like in your lungs."

With that thought foremost, he lunged out the sliding door at Fargo's Hector International Airport and sucked in a long pull of air. He gagged, he coughed, and staggered toward the Enclave. We laughed when he told us the full story.

"Real Minnesotans train themselves to take a huge breath *before* they walk outside," we teased. "And we hold it until we get to the car!"

The weekend of family, games, friends, and ringing in the new year was such a blessing. Our last holiday with Randy and the first with Mitchell.

A few months later, Mitchell phoned Randy to ask permission to marry his daughter. It was a sweet and emotional conversation for both of them. Randy was thrilled and only asked that Mitchell take good care of our daughter.

I already knew what was in the works. Randy had given me a heads-up when he texted:

> *Randy: Okay, I can't keep a secret. Mitchell is calling me around 4:30 today. I think it's a Wilkin Burger night after that.*
> *Me: How did you find out? I'm freaking out! Does Emily know?*

Randy: He sent me a text this morning.
Me: Cool, he's making brownie points with me ☺
Randy: YOU'RE freaking out? I'm the one on the
hot seat ☺
Me: What will your answer be?
Randy: What should it be? (Duh)
Me: He has my blessing as long as he remembers part of
her heart will always be in MN and she needs to stay an
active participant in this state. Whatever that means!
Randy: I said no. Joking!

With Randy's permission and my blessing, Mitchell
planned every last detail as he plotted to pop the question to Emily.
To our delight, he thoughtfully included Randy and me in the
special moment.

Recalling that Emily had vacationed at Sanibel Island—her
"happy place"—with grandparents and family, he convinced her to
spend spring break with us in Florida.

After a week of soaking in sun, sand, and water, Mitchell
organized a day trip to Emily's favorite, Sanibel Lighthouse Beach.

When he invited her on a romantic walk by the surf,
Randy and I decided to head out for a walk as well. Except Emily
was not in the mood for a romantic walk. So, halfway down the
beach Mitchell suggested they make a sandcastle. Without tools,
their sandcastle wasn't going to win any awards, but it served his
purpose. When it was finished, they strolled on.

In the meantime, Randy and I made our way along the same
path. We stayed well-hidden to accomplish the secret tasks Mitchell
had assigned. Entrusted with the engagement ring, Randy carefully
placed it on top of the sandcastle. My job was to wait, photograph,
and video record the proposal. We kept our eyes on the large birds
circling above—wary that they would swoop down and steal the
sparkling ring.

Right on cue, Mitchell and Emily returned, pausing near the

sandcastle. He stopped short. When she turned, Mitchell was down on one knee. There were several loud screams, tears of joy, a pause.

"Yes, I'll marry you!" Her joyous response bounced along the beach.

After lots of hugs, we all headed back to the waterfront where the rest of the family waited, wondering what on earth was happening. Suspicious all along, Matthew and Tyler were peeved that they weren't part of Emily's surprise, but they were excited to see her engagement ring.

It might have been easy to worry about the timing or question their decision, yet Randy and I knew, deep down, that God was in control of their relationship.

The rest of that spring and summer, the kids made several trips back to Minnesota, enriching our family, strengthening our bonds—and allowing Randy and Mitchell time to get to know each other. A true blessing-in-disguise as God began to prepare us for our unthinkable future.

Randy's death.

Suddenly, the focus changed in the most unfortunate way possible and wedding plans came to a staggering and abrupt halt. For the immediate months following his funeral, no one mentioned the wedding. When it felt right to revisit the topic, the tone, mood, and plans changed dramatically.

My attention needed to focus and center on helping Emily plan. The bride and groom chose to honor and remember Randy on their wedding day. Everything we planned and everything we decided was through a lens of Emily without her dad at her wedding—a huge elephant-in-the-room for both the wedding party and the guests.

With the aim of substituting joy for sorrow, Emily intentionally designed elements to include her dad's memory. In Randy's stead, her older brother Tyler would walk her down the aisle. The ceremony included moments to honor Randy, as well.

The reception and dance, too, were considered. As a little

girl, Emily dreamed about her daddy-daughter dance and years earlier had picked the perfect song—Stephen Curtis Chapman's "Cinderella." She'd just been waiting for Mr. Right to come along. Now, she had him … but no daddy for the song. A painful reality.

Anticipating this as the most painful moment of her wedding, she engaged Jared and Shawn, two talented musicians and close college friends of hers—to write and perform a new song. Just for her and Mitchell. They would perform the song while she danced with several important men in her life: her grandfather Gene, her brothers, Tyler and Matthew; her godfather, Jim; Randy's brother, Steve; close family friend John, her father-in-law, Mitch; and her new husband, Mitchell.

Although her dad was not there to dance to their song, Emily was able to pay tribute to him through those who played supporting roles after his death. As hard as the day was without Randy, we made the best of it and tried to honor him in the highest ways we knew. There were many moments of joy and happiness offset by some tender moments of loss and longing.

That night we lounged around a campfire with just family and a few close friends, recapping the day and talking about Randy and how proud he would have been of Emily and Mitchell. We ended the night with a lantern release, a symbol of sending our hugs and love to heaven. It was Emily's way of saying, "Thank you, Dad." A bittersweet day in the midst of our grief.

Twenty-six

Just one week later, we again moved into graduation mode to celebrate the end of Matthew's twelve years at Breckenridge schools. Seeing another child walk across a stage, Randy notably absent, pierced deeply. Especially since this was our last child to graduate from high school.

The end of a parenting era, for sure.

Family surrounded us and cheered loudly as Matthew crossed the threshold and accepted his signed diploma. He did it!

We did it.

We survived.

The event-packed months had passed, leaving me exhausted. Strained by the never-ending decisions. Hazy about all had transpired.

So much had changed so quickly. Yet, at the end of the day, there was little control I had on any of the timing of it. God was in control. The timing was *His*.

And thankfully so. If I had had it *my* way, nothing would have changed that first year until we felt stronger. But God knew what He was doing; those changes brought us all exactly where He wanted us.

Twenty-seven

The loss of Randy, I was learning, had changed me. As I began to understand myself, Jana without Randy, I discovered that the person I was … was here to stay. The new me also had to maneuver through the changes this created in my relationships.

This was most obvious with my kids.

Each one of my children processed their grief in their own way. The boys, by working through a lot of their grief internally. Our phone calls centered on hearing each other's voices and catching up on the day or life events—never about their feelings or talking about how much they missed their dad. Our face-to-face interactions informed me enough to know they were dealing with their pain, but not in a verbal way. At least not with their mother.

Emily, however, was more external with her processing. When she wasn't in tears or telling me how sad she was, I was telling her about my own loneliness. With the first "hello" of a phone call, I knew whether it would be a joyful or sad conversation.

Often, I heard only silence until I would ask, "Emily, are you okay?"

She was crying, simply needing to hear her mom's voice.

One weekend when we were all together, I sensed that the kids were at different stages in their grief—especially evident on one of our walks. Tyler and Emily had been bickering back and forth when suddenly Tyler lashed out at his sister.

"Emily, you're not the only one who lost a dad!" he yelled. "He was my dad too."

Naturally, his outburst was not graciously received and a heated exchange followed. Eventually, they were able to talk it out and settle down, but I took note, observing how differently they were processing their loss.

It pained my heart to witness their raw emotions being expressed this way, but I knew I had to let it go, allow them to speak their minds. I couldn't fix it. I couldn't control it. It had to come out.

Most importantly, we all stayed connected, talking openly about Randy and how our grief journeys were changing our lives from the inside out. Then came a time when we all became apprehensive about being verbal with our grief … because none of us wanted to make the others sad. Of course each of us had Randy on our mind and wanted so badly to speak openly, but no one wanted to make it worse for the others.

Although I tried to wear a happy face for their sakes, I was grateful my kids couldn't see the emotions flashing across my face during so many phone conversations. I did my best to act like I had it all together when I really wanted to ask, "How are you honestly feeling today? How are you managing your life with this huge hole in it? Do you miss your dad as much as I do?"

If I was honest with myself, I feared their answers. *And,* I fretted, *they may not want to truthfully tell me.*

Several weeks after their wedding, just after Matthew's graduation party, Emily and Mitchell prepared to return to Nashville and start their married life. While they loaded the U-Haul with gifts and items from her bedroom, I overheard Emily snap at Mitchell for being cheap and not renting a larger trailer to cart it all.

Feeling the tension, I tried my best to calm her down and encourage Mitchell to stay the course. "Keep loading. You'll both feel better once you get on the road."

Much of the emotion, I knew, stemmed from the abrupt descent from the mountain-top high of the wedding and their honeymoon trip to Mexico. The all-inclusive resort with beverages galore, endless food choices, and swimming with the dolphins—a bucket-list event for Emily—had kept her occupied and euphoric. Until this moment.

Something in my gut me told me there was more to this outburst than stress or that Mitchell had planned things a little too tightly. I felt a nudge from God: "Trust Me, Jana. It's going to be okay."

Mitchell continued to carefully pack the trailer, using every possible inch. When I noticed Emily wasn't around, I went looking for her. I couldn't find her anywhere. "Mitchell, have you seen Emily?" "Nope," he said. "Not sure where she went."

Time ticked by and still no Emily. Eventually Matthew came outside. "Did you know Emily's on the floor of her closet? Sleeping?"

After suffering a crippling anxiety attack, she'd fallen asleep in that tiny space.

The newlyweds left hours later than planned, the trailer stuffed full and the back seat crammed with childhood mementos. Emily had moved out and was moving on with her life as a married woman.

That week we checked in often. With each conversation, I could sense something amiss. Her voice sounded weak and tired, her mood seemed off. Our phone conversations felt forced. It ate at me. What was wrong? Had the wedding happened too soon after Randy's death? Should they have waited?

Several weeks after they settled into their Brentwood

apartment just south of Nashville, I got a troubling phone call from my new son-in-law. His voice was soft but shaken.

"Emily has been having irrational behaviors over the past few days," he confided, "to the point where I am concerned for her safety."

My heart felt as though an elephant had parked itself right in the middle of my chest. What was happening to us? Why was God continuing to challenge us like this?

Mitchell went on to help me understand what had precipitated him taking her to the ER. She had started having irrational fears and couldn't stop from crying. "She scared me. I felt like only a doctor could help," he said.

The emergency room sent her for a consultation with the psychologist, who determined hospitalization would be best for Emily, for her safety and Mitchell's sanity.

My daughter had suffered a breakdown and eventually was diagnosed with post-traumatic stress disorder—PTSD. Her body had emotionally shut down and the events of the past year had caught up to her. She was broken.

Living 1100 miles apart, we were a world away from each other. My baby was sick, and I wasn't there with her. She was in the hospital, and I couldn't care for her. What kind of mother was I?

Mitchell assured me that he was with her and, even if I were there, I couldn't see her right now. The inpatient care program allowed her only thirty minutes a day with one family member. That person needed to be her husband, I reminded myself, not me.

I still beat myself up.

I should have been there for her. I should have seen this coming. I should have talked to her more, taken her to see someone, expressed my concern ....

Praying ferociously for the next hours and days, I sought peace. *Peace in my heart, dear Lord. This is just too much. Like losing a husband wasn't enough, now my daughter is in serious trouble with her mental health.*

Why God? Why now?

God granted me the peace I needed so desperately, an unbelievable amount of peace. Like a gentle breeze brushing across me, calmness sifted over my heart and mind.

Trust Me, Jana. I've got this. How many times would I need to hear that?

I found myself in a more relaxed state than I had been in months. Oh, I still cried over Randy and my children and myself. I was still concerned with Emily's mental health, but the sense of utter peace that passed over me was something only God could provide. *Trust* ... the word took away the worry from those dark days of Emily's broken heartedness. I surrendered my fears to God.

Hearing my daughter's voice the first time she was allowed to call was a sincere relief. Her voice was shaky and she spoke softly, but she said with deep sincerity that she loved and missed me. I had all I really needed at that moment.

The words from my friend Marcia rang in my head over and over again: "You're only as happy as your saddest kid."

We had been talking over our routine "shake" lunch when I told her about Emily.

"Jana, you need to go and see her, even if it's only for a few minutes. You need to do this for you. For your own reassurance."

Taking her motherly advice, I booked a ticket to Nashville.

The week she was released from the hospital to the outpatient program, I spent several days with Emily in their apartment. Driving her to and from outpatient classes, doing her laundry and all those mom-like duties, just being with her helped my soul. Daily, I sought God's hand in leading me and continuing to encourage me to give it up to Him. When I continued to release my worry, my peace grew incrementally.

Trust, I was beginning to see, equals peace.

While Emily worked hard to climb out of her gloomy abyss—a journey that would take her several years, I continued to find solace as I handed every concern to Him. Worry dissipated and my sleepless nights turned themselves around.

As I questioned the timing of Emily's breakdown and the ultimate timing of Randy's death, I reconciled in my mind that God's timing is not the question. Trusting God means His timing is perfect. Trusting His timing means I have the sure knowledge that everything will make sense.

In His time.

Twenty-eight

It was intimidating and scary when I thought about being the only surviving parent. A grave responsibility. I knew I had to stay safe. I needed to do all I could to remain healthy.

I can't die and leave them as orphans!

That sounded a tad dramatic, I felt, but a terrifying reality surfaced: My kids, too, feared something happening to me. Randy's death was so unexpected and unplanned; it shook them to their core to think that I might also die at any moment.

"I wish we could all live in a bubble. Safe and together, where nothing bad will happen to any of us again," Emily said one day.

"Oh, honey, that's not how life works," I reminded her gently.

"But, what if something happens to you?"

All of my kids would have to work through this natural concern in their own ways. Time and time again, I received texts and phone calls making sure I was okay. Making sure I was safe. Making sure I was alive. And I reciprocated.

"If you don't answer my text or your phone when I call," I would say, "the mother in me assumes you're dead in a ditch. Be kind. Be considerate. Answer your phone!"

Truthfully, I found an odd comfort in knowing they were keeping an eye on me—as I was on them. Who else was there now to know, or care, if I didn't arrive home okay at night?

As his wife, I had relied on Randy to worry about me, keep track of me. He was my personal safety net. I could always count on him to keep a watchful eye on me. Now, my kids were paying close attention to my comings and goings.

It was reassuring.

But the unfamiliar weight of solo parenting settled heavily on my shoulders.

Randy and I were a team in the best possible way. Parenting was a joint effort. A partnership. We fully relied on each other to help raise the kids, bouncing things off each other—curfews, permission to stay over at friends, the normal stuff.

Now that he was gone, I was left to try to make the best possible decisions for them. *Alone.* And I had absolutely no practice in parenting alone. Suddenly the two- heads-are-better-than-one theory was out the window. Now it was only me, my thoughts, my decisions. No matter what problem might arise.

Like calls from the kids asking guidance about a relational issue—without Randy's input. Or conversations seeking advice for their future: Should he buy this house or that new car? I had done the same as a young adult, calling my parents for their counsel on big decisions. But my kids would have to be satisfied with my puny advice-from-one, my uncertain solo response.

It was a strange and frightening spot to find myself.

I remembered when my parents had to face the death of their parents; they both commented how weird it felt to not have them around anymore for guidance. Families are designed with parents and spouses for you to look to for advice and for counsel. When they are gone, it rocks our world and shakes us to our core.

A winding road passed before my eyes, filled with intersections and traffic jams. Could I navigate it? Could I carry the responsibility of parental decisions completely on my own?

I had lost my confidence without Randy.

Twenty-nine

Couple friends, single friends, my friends, your friends.
Who knew friendship could be so complicated?

I realized early on that some of the friendships Randy and
I shared needed to be explored now that I was single. Some couple
friends were just that, friends we saw as a couple; others were
individual relationships inside of being a couple. Even though many
made a point to say, "Nothing is going to change," the reality was:
How could it not?

The first holiday season portrayed a stark picture of my life
in the coming months. As I floundered in our crowd of friends, I
began to understand the significant change that had to take place in
those relationships.

Our drive to social events had afforded Randy and I prep
time to speculate on who might attend and what might be happening
their lives. During the ride home, we rehashed the party—a personal
conversation between us as trusted confidants. No judging, just

laughter and reassessing the night's festivities.

One evening after Randy's death, friends invited me to a holiday party at their home. The guests included a hodge-podge of friends from various circles of my life. Marcia and John anticipated my discomfort and insisted on chauffeuring me even though I lived well out of their way. We joined the already assembled crew, which included several with whom Randy and I had often associated in our free time. But, on this night, a crucial guest was missing. The spot at my side was vacant. My eyes darted to the doorway, to each corner of the room, always looking for The One Who Was Absent.

The chatter was lively, the conversation light. Everything was as it should be, acquaintances enjoying some holiday cheer, talking about upcoming Christmas plans. Yet the casual, nonchalant conversation caused pangs of uneasiness deep within me. These were our people, friends I should have felt good being around. Instead, I felt lonely and unsettled. Deeply saddened.

How can they be thinking about Christmas? How can they talk like everything is normal? Like life will continue on?

No one could have predicted my reaction; no one foresaw the awkwardness I would feel as only half a couple. We were all navigating unchartered waters, holiday parties without Randy.

Too soon, too soon! my damaged soul insisted.

When Marcia sensed my heartache, she suggested we leave earlier than planned. The return trip was quiet, a blunt contrast to the light-hearted homeward drives with Randy.

After that night, I no longer automatically accepted social invitations. Future outings, I vowed, would involve strategy on my part. To that end, I asked vital questions: Who would attend? How many? Were these people I knew? Trying to anticipate how I might react on those occasions, I took time to consider each circumstance, which allowed me to create a safe space where I could be myself, let my guard down, stop looking for The Missing Guest. Where it didn't feel like the world was racing along, but rather where I could catch my breath, relax. I was best served with rather small crowds where I could visit and interact more intimately.

As the months passed, I grew stronger, aware that I was becoming a new version of myself, riding into my new norm. My interests expanded and broadened. My free time centered on doing things I rarely considered when Randy was living.

My sister Kathy, who lives almost four hours away, became one of my favorite people to hang out with. Growing up, playing endless hours of dolls, school, and pretend, we developed tight bonds. Oh, we had our fights and disagreements, but first and always, we were sisters. Our youngest sister Susan had died in a car/bike accident when she was five, which drew us even closer. We had only each other as sisters.

Kathy and I attended one year of college together—she as a freshman, I as a senior—where our relationship deepened to true friendship. Then we went our separate ways, found our spouses, and started our families. Sure, we spent holidays and many weekends at the lake together, but we drifted a bit from our sisterhood.

That all changed when Randy died. My sister became and remains my confidant, my go-to person who shares my deep, dark secrets.

"I don't have Randy to tell everything to, so now you get to listen to it all," I tease.

Unlike my kids or my friends, Kathy can't and won't run from my hardest days. I'm grateful and thank God often for her— my sister-friend.

• • • • • • •

When Randy was alive, we spent most weekends with our kids, doing family activities like biking, hiking, traveling. I needed to test drive new ideas to fill those hours we had spent together. During this time, I expanded my hobbies to include more things I could do alone or with a friend.

I increased my knowledge and passion for basketball by

attending many of the local games. My friend Diane's husband, Dick, was a basketball coach, so she became my buddy-on-the-bench. An outdoor-loving couple, they often included me in their outings and activities.

Randy had been a basketball player, and, in fact, was on the team the last time Breckenridge Cowboys advanced to the Minnesota state tournament. Ironically, I'd waited until now to invest myself in the sport. Possibly in his memory. In some strange way, learning more about basketball, *his* sport, made me feel closer to him.

That season the Cowboys advanced to the state tournament, the first time since 1979. Spectators bought commemorative tee-shirts to promote the team. Listed on the backside were the names of all the team players. And there, at the bottom … *Randy Berndt.* There was a strong connection between the team and Randy's memory, especially evident when, at the section championship game, the coach made his way over to greet me and acknowledge my attendance. We embraced as he thanked me for my support.

Additionally, season tickets to college basketball in Fargo were a good buy for Matthew and I. Now a Bison men's basketball sports nut, I looked forward to our mother-son outings over the long winter months and our time with the Richman family, whose son coached the team.

During those short days and early nights, my reading grew legs as I no longer pored over strictly work-related books but began choosing topics purely out of interest or curiosity. When spring arrived, I expanded my gardening skills by trying my hand at growing flowers, greenery, and apples.

I even made new friends, some whom were single, some whose husbands were gone a bit in the evenings. Now I had companions willing to catch a movie with me or join me for dinner at a restaurant.

Stretching my neck outside my own little world, I focused some attention on Irva, Marcia's aging mother who had recently moved to an assisted living facility in Breckenridge. Also widowed at a young age, Irva warmed to me when I reached out and invited her to dinner regularly. She welcomed the change of scenery and I enjoyed the change of pace. Laughter punctuated our visits, but she also educated me on the dos and don'ts of widowhood during our many heartwarming conversations. She'd been there and done that.

Most importantly, I made friends with Jana-the-single-woman. She was home alone. Teaching herself to become comfortable in her own skin. I learned to spend time with her, with myself ... by myself. To cook for one. Eat with one. And attend functions as one. This meant exploring a friendship with myself.

Many of my friendships shifted. They changed. Some grew stronger, some became seasonal, some dissolved. It's the truth and it's hard–hard for all involved. No one can put a finger on the "why;" no one knows whether some of the friendships will reappear. It just happens.

I released myself from the guilt and pain of this reality. I prayed for God's wisdom and guidance as I gained peace over these relationships. Those new *and* those renewed.

Thirty

A not-so-surprising discovery had dawned on me: No two paths of grieving are the same. No one else could experience the identical emotional rollercoaster I rode. My loss was my loss. My grief was my grief. The story was mine and Randy's alone.

Well-meaning people often said, "I know exactly what you are going through."

While this was not helpful in the moment, I reconciled myself with the understanding that they offered their best. This was their attempt to empathize and comfort me in my devastation. But the reality was, there was no way for them to fully understand my grief. Just like I couldn't understand someone else's bereavement.

Others said, "God gained another angel. Randy's in a better place."

A better place? Really, I think our life in Breckenridge was a pretty awesome place!

The most comforting words that I wanted to hear early on

were, "I'm sorry for your loss." Period. No more, no less. Just a simple, "I'm sorry." It goes a long way to salve a crushed heart.

Of course, I understood their intentions were pure.

Even so ....

The days and weeks moved along and I stumbled over another discovery: Not only is our grief our own, we all accept loss at various paces.

During a catch-up phone call with a friend, she admitted, "I'm angry at God for taking Randy from us."

A light bulb went off in my head at the realization that she and I were at very different steps in our grief. She was hurt, upset at losing a friend. I did not feel the same anger she expressed; anger was not an emotion I had yet encountered. But I recognized it as part of others' wayfaring through the degrees of mourning.

Understanding my kids' acceptance of losing their dad was another story.

I couldn't think of any part of parenting more difficult than seeing my children so desperately hurt. My momma bear instinct was to take away the intense and deep pain they endured. I wanted to bear the pain for them. Each time I saw a tear or witnessed an out lash of emotion, I begged God to take their pain away and give it all to me.

I longed for Emily to have her father walk her down the aisle on her wedding day. I would have done anything to have Randy witness Matthew's walk across the stage to receive his diploma. And how I yearned to have Randy at my side when I got a phone call from Tyler about his car accident just a few weeks after his father's death.

Just as my grief was my own, their grief was theirs.

They had lost their dad and there wasn't anything I could do to change or take that away. They needed to grieve their father and I needed to let them, just as they needed to let me grieve my husband.

Each of us took our time to fully feel and move through our loss. I tended to hide my deepest, darkest emotions from them so as to not burden them with another load to carry. Emily and I moved along differently than Tyler and Matthew. I sensed frustration between the boys and their sister as she struggled outwardly much longer than they did.

Get over it. Just move on. Other similar phrases passed their lips, impatient as they were with their sister's more obvious grief. Often in haste, sometimes in despair, as they more privately worked their own. This is not to say that the boys didn't struggle or miss their dad, but their outward appearance was subdued and somewhat of a mystery to me.

Grief appeared in unexpected ways. Short tempers, irrational anger, flares of frustration at odd moments. It all added up to a much needed act of grace. None of us could really hold each other accountable for changes in temperaments or untimely mood swings during those dark months. I chalked it up to individual, one-of-a-kind grief.

In March, Matthew and I took a little getaway to Florida to visit my parents. On the plane ride down to Estero, we were absorbed by the music in our earphones. I noticed a tear slipping down Matthew's cheek.

No words were exchanged. Instead, I closed my eyes.

God, I silently prayed, *please encourage Matthew through this troubling time. Let him feel peace with his dad's death and memory.*

It was a rare moment with my son, an unintentional reminder that he, too, was dealing with sorrow in his own way.

Thirty-one

"Forrest Gump" was one of Randy's all-time favorite movies. After watching it at least two dozen times, he could quote most of the dialogue. Through the years, I was the audience to whom he performed those famous lines.

Each spring he would quote, "*That's my boat.*"

The summer after he died, a huge burden hung over me: What should we do about Randy's beloved boat?

Growing up in Minnesota—the Land of Ten Thousand Lakes—and spending a fair amount of time at said lakes had given Randy and me an appreciation for boating and water sports. When Randy was younger, he and his brothers pooled their hard-earned money to buy a first speedboat. It brought the boys many hours of entertainment, and gave Randy the opportunity to become an excellent water skier.

About ten years into our marriage, we made a big investment into boat ownership and purchased a speedboat of our own. We didn't own a lot on a lake, but we did have a vehicle, a hitch, and trailer, which was all we needed to haul the *Mariah* around the area to enjoy many Minnesota and Wisconsin lakes.

Boating provided great family time in the summers. Skiing, tubing, wakeboarding, or simply cruising on a Sunday afternoon—it didn't take much for us to have fun. This is the main reason you consider living in Minnesota: for the summers at the lake.

When Randy was in his boat, he was on top of the world. He had a kind of joy inside that only came from *his* boat. He loved everything about it—cleaning, buffing, tinkering with, parking, and driving the *Mariah*.

The *Mariah* would give us several great years of boating and family memories until we traded her for the *Larson*. A bit of a downsize, but necessary when Randy went back to college to get his teaching degree. It still brought Randy all the joy needed to enjoy Minnesota summers.

One summer, we attached the tubes to the back of the boat and the three kids eagerly hopped on. With Randy at the wheel, the ride was always a little more exciting than with me. So naturally, Randy was the driver and I was the spotter. Camera in hand, I hoped to journal the kids' joy ride.

That was my first mistake.

After capturing lots of big waves and squeals of laughter and delight, I noticed Tyler and Emily waving their arms and yelling at me.

They're really having fun. I smiled into the viewfinder. I kept shooting and the boat kept going.

That was my second, bigger mistake.

Eventually, I noticed only two kids through the lens. What? Where was that third kid?

Where's Matthew?

My head bobbed up and I scanned the lake for my youngest son. I eventually spotted him in the middle of the lake. When he had fallen off his tube, the other two had been waving and yelling to tell me. Randy turned the boat and headed back to collect him. All turned out fine and nothing was lost except maybe a little of my ego. How could I have left my baby in the middle of the lake?

We had many laughs about that tubing ride. I tried to take it all like a good sport. The kids still tease me about my spotting skills, that if given the choice they would pick someone else for the job.

The story, along with countless others, still warmed my heart. Our family had made an abundance of precious memories on the lake.

Now, it was impossible to imagine being on board without Randy.

What to do about it all?

By this time, we had purchased the lake place with extended family; there was a place for the boat, a permanent summer spot in a lift. Remembering that boating with his brothers became synonymous with joyous family time for Randy—something he was determined to bring to a family of his own … well, how could we *not* continue the legacy?

The kids and I decided to hitch up, haul it to its new home, and park it.

Emotions gushed and I floundered in the wave of it all.

I kept hearing my husband's voice and seeing the huge smile he always wore when he sat in the driver's seat. The rush of memories made me ache to see that same smile once again. How could something as worldly as a boat remind me so deeply of what I had lost?

I felt inadequate for the situation.

What if it doesn't start? What if I don't land it right? What will it feel like to take over Randy's boat?

The first official ride was hard. But we survived. Another first among the many of firsts we'd had and would continue to have. We drove it, we landed it, and we started a new chapter with Randy's boat.

Each time I took the boat out, it became a little easier, and we started to reclaim some of the exuberance we once shared with Randy, in his pride and joy.

Thirty-two

Disbelief, sadness, worry, and fear seemed inherent to my abrupt widowhood. Prayers, petitions, and conversations typically centered around one of these emotions.

One of the most vividly real and tough emotions I experienced was feeling scared. Scared to a point that it kept me frozen in my thoughts and I could barely move forward.

The first weekend that I was home alone was terrifying. It had been almost thirty years since I had been alone at night. I thought I had done my best to plan ahead for this moment, but nothing could prepare me for the 2:00 a.m. alarm inside of me that went off, reminding me of how alone I was.

Why do things always seem so major in the middle of the night?

Worry began to consume me. I worried about the future without Randy. The thought of living alone was too, too much to think about. I worried about finances. I worried about single parenting. I worried about things real and things imagined. I worried for the sake of worrying.

I never volunteered for this title of Widow. No way.

It hung heavy and loose, unfamiliar. Like a winter coat someone insists is yours. It was uncomfortable and it didn't fit and I didn't like it and I didn't want it.

So many concerns, so many emotions roiled through me. Thankfully, dawn chased away my dark thoughts.

Morning light brought the memory of another time I'd had a brush with widowhood.

In 2002 Randy was diagnosed with a meningioma brain tumor that had been removed, thankfully. A paralyzing fear of losing my husband during surgery swept over me, even though we were given a relatively hopeful diagnosis.

Because the surgery was successful, there were no real issues of concern. Doctors prescribed an anti-seizure medicine as a precaution. Randy took it diligently—the first few months—with no issues or frightening side effects.

As time went along, his faithfulness slipped. Some days he forgot all together. This didn't seem to overly concern his doctors. After all, many brain surgery patients begin weaning off the medication after a few months, provided everything in their test results looks normal.

Several years later on July 3, we were boating at the lake. I was pulling Randy on the water tube when, with no warning, he let go of the tube and fell face down into the water. His life jacket brought his body to the surface but there was no sign of movement.

My heart sank and my pulse began to pound as I turned and drove the boat as fast as I could to where my husband bobbed, still face down, no oxygen supply and no sign of life. Emily, who was only ten at the time, already had her life jacket over her shoulders and was poised at the front of the boat ready to dive in after her dad. One of the strongest swimmers in our family, she had no fear of the water and took off as soon as she was within swimming distance.

I stopped the boat quickly. My dad threw a life jacket to me and I strapped myself into it. I was not at all a swimmer, in fact, I'm quite terrified of the water, but without thought I jumped in after Emily.

I had no idea what had happened to Randy but I had a sinking feeling in my stomach that this wasn't good. I never imagined losing him, not like this, and not this soon.

Oh, dear Lord, please do not make me a widow. I can't do life alone, not without Randy. Please, God, not now.

By the time I got to him, his lips had turned blue and he was not breathing. I pulled and tugged on his life jacket until he finally started to show signs of wanting to breathe. His lips started to pink-up a bit. It seemed like he was going to breathe on his own.

By God's grace, a nearby pontoon raced over when the driver saw we were in trouble. The boaters were able to lift Randy onto the front of their boat. We were unaware at the time that two medical professionals onboard knew what to do.

By the time they got him to shore, Randy was breathing and starting to come around. An ambulance waited on the beach and took him to the local hospital where he spent the night under observation. He had had a grand mal seizure. Doctors put Randy back on his anti-seizure medicine and all was good for Independence Day the next morning.

After that experience, I never imagined that only ten years later I would beg God again not to make me a widow.

Determined more than ever to find tools to help me, I reached for an article by Catherine Woodiwiss. "This is the big, scary thing about trauma: there is no such thing as 'getting over it.' The five stages of the grief model," she wrote, "marks universal stages in learning to accept loss, but the reality is in fact much bigger: a major life disruption leaves a new normal in its wake. There is not 'back to the old me.' You are different now."

A powerful *aha* moment struck me. I needed to personalize my path in order to move forward as a widow. I had already come to a place where I redefined the stages of grief for myself. She was right. There was no going back to the "old me."

This was a woman I could understand and relate to! I read on: "This is not a wholly negative thing. Healing from trauma can also mean finding a new strength and joy. The goal of healing is not a papering-over the changes in an effort to preserve or present things as normal. It is to acknowledge and wear your new life—warts, wisdom, and all—with courage."

To acknowledge and wear my "new life." Powerful.

I didn't want my identity to include Widow. But that was a part of my story, and while it didn't define me, being a widow in this season of life was part of my identity.

Like someone in a twelve-step program, I admitted to the room, "I am Jana Berndt and I am a widow."

The coat wasn't as loose as I'd thought.

A small measure of acceptance and peace settled over me. A huge piece of this was letting go of who I was and discovering who I was becoming. I had to stop looking for my old self and find my new self. Me, without Randy.

I knew I would never truly "be over it," but I could wear this new life—with courage.

Thirty-three

Sympathy cards, food and casseroles, thank-you notes, funeral processionals—so many funeral traditions and rituals society has embraced for generations. And, as friends and neighbors, we do it all so well. During our personal tragedy, I pondered: *Is all this really as helpful as we intend it to be?*

I was touched and humbled by the outpouring of love and support we received. But my gratitude was overshadowed by my absorption of keeping track of each kindness so that we could eventually acknowledge and properly thank all those wonderful people who stepped forward to help.

Thank-you notes. And so many of them. How will I find and gather all the addresses we'll need to mail them?

I was in no state to begin writing, but my conscience got the best of me. Mere days after the funeral I started the daunting task. As I penned each one, I recalled my grandma's gentle coaching during my youth to acknowledge the generosity and thoughtfulness of others. Birthday and Christmas presents, graduation and wedding gifts.

But she never talked about the obligation of note writing during the season of mourning.

Bounteous food appeared, filling every crevice of the refrigerator and freezer, piling up on the countertops and overflowing to a few tables eventually set up in the garage. Annette and a few other friends took on the time-consuming job of coordinating all the calls about dropping off food.

Let me be clear. Our family was grateful for everything. Each kind deed!

If directly asked, I would have insisted, "We're fine. We don't need food."

It's a good thing I wasn't asked. The burden of shopping and meal preparation would have been too much for us. Thank goodness others saw our need. We would have starved had it not been for our generous friends. It's just that our appetite and interest was not equal to the amount of food that filled our house. Simple protein shakes were often the most we could handle. Our appetites wouldn't really return until months later—when the hot dishes were long, long gone.

I'd been on the other side, of course, and had always felt that bringing food was a gesture that the family needed and certainly wanted. But how many families need one hundred casseroles or twenty dozen bar cookies delivered the week of the funeral? How much more sensible if this quantity of food was delivered over a period of months rather than days?

But how, exactly, does a genuinely grateful widow suggest something like that? I mused.

Had my mind and emotions been less shredded by grief, I might have asked someone to coordinate such a venture. But everything had come so fast and furiously and, frankly, organizing anything at this moment was too much to handle.

Food, the international sign of concern. The safe way to

support a family in need. An excuse to show up, check on the family, spread hugs around, and make sure everything is going to be okay.

It was dawning on me that there is no one-size-fits-all approach to assisting and comforting the bereaved. But, surely, there was a better way than a deluge of dishes?

More than thank-you notes, what I really wanted to do was rewrite the long-standing tradition of casseroles.

All of this caused me to revisit my own traditions.

I would, of course, wait a month or more to deliver a meal. Wait until the mourning family was adjusting to their new norm. Who is really going to feel like cooking when the adjustment is so painful? They might even lose interest in some of the household duties. Day-to-day life is a real challenge after a loss.

I was determined to pause a while, to wait a bit before sending my own sympathy cards. Even several months later, I was learning, a family might need the extra encouragement of hearing from a friend. And the memorial money I might send would be something the family contemplates for weeks, months, or even years after the loss of their loved one. Waiting just a few weeks wouldn't change any of that. When cards arrived weeks after Randy's death, I was touched that others still had us on their hearts.

Another idea I wanted to incorporate was random acts of kindness. I knew how it felt to be on the receiving end of the thoughtful neighbors who stopped by to rake my leaves or mow my grass or simply drop off a case of bottled water.

I recalled the day my friend Perry stopped by and offered to take home the laundry. His wife Denise knew we had extended family staying with us and probably had mounds of dirty towels and bedding. She washed and dried them, returning them the same day. That profound, yet simple gesture relieved my mind of one basic household task.

And Paul, our neighbor across the street, offered his house to my brother's family during the funeral. The local hotels, it turned out, were booked because of a hockey tournament in town that weekend. Paul was in the process of selling and had already moved out most of his things. He opened his entire house to our family throughout the week. A thoughtful act of kindness we hadn't realized we needed.

Small deeds, I was learning, have a big impact on a family paralyzed by grief. I prayed to be sensitive to the needs of others in their times of distress.

Thirty-four

Randy was a friend to many throughout his life, but there was a special bond between him and our golden retriever, Max. It's often said that a dog is a man's best friend and this held true for Randy and Max, who were BFFs and spent a lot of time together on walks and runs.

Some refer to their dog as their protector, helper, lifesaver, and companion—true for these two. And Max was there for when Randy needed him most: his companion on the run when he collapsed. Typically, Max would've darted off in a game of catch-me-if-you-can.

That morning, Max stayed faithfully at Randy's side until help arrived.

I've never been a "dog-person" or an animal lover at all. When I was young, our family owned a dog named Skipper. Let's just say that his stay in the Sipe household was short-lived. My mom was not a dog person either.

Our kids were barely old enough to spell *d-o-g* before they started begging for a pet. We tried to satisfy them with a fish aquarium, which kept them occupied–for a while.

"Pleeeeeease, Mom. We *need* a dog. We'll do all the work." Their promises continued: "We'll feed it. We'll walk it. We'll ....."

They wore us down and we bought a shih tzu from a local breeder, so we would be certain he was a purebred. We named him Tiger and he lived up to his name.

Like all puppies, he was adorable when we first got him. Then reality smacked us in the face as we started the work of training. Tiger had a bit of a mean streak and we quickly realized he was not the friendliest family dog. With a household of young kids who wanted to play with him and pet him, we knew Tiger needed a family better suited to his personality.

A few years later we got a cat, Cassie, followed by another cat, Charlie. Dog people understand a cat doesn't really replace a desire for a dog, and our kids were no different. Eventually, an adorable golden retriever came to live with the Berndts. As much as I did not want another pet, whatsoever, Max came as divine intervention.

In the spring of 2010, Tyler called from college to tell us he was thinking about staying in St. Cloud for the summer.

"What? You're not coming home?" I'd already anticipated boating at the lake and all the fun we'd have as a family. "Uh, let's talk about this."

We discussed his options and what might be most sensible. Knowing me well, Tyler played to my weakness.

"You know," he offered at one point, "I'd come home for sure—if we could get a dog."

To this day, I'm still not one hundred percent positive the kids weren't co-conspiring behind my back. It didn't take much at all for him to get Emily on board to pay for the dog. Obviously, my hands were tied.

Tyler was the politician, but Emily became the CEO over

Max since she was the one to buy him, Matthew the COO over day-to-day operations, Jana the CFO funding day-to-day operations, and Randy the BFF and true caregiver.

We took lots of pictures to document Max's puppyhood and all that puppy cuteness. To this day, my favorite family professional photo is when Max was just a few months old. Why can't they stay cute and small just a little longer?

Safe to say, Max turned me into a dog-person—or, at least, a Max-the-golden-retriever-person. If you asked my Buck Saw Lodge family, including my mom, they too would say Max is impossible not to love.

After Randy's collapse, poor Max wasn't able to be at the hospital with us right away. In fact, when we arrived at the scene to find Max in the police car, we phoned our neighbor Brian to pick him up. He eventually went to the kennel. Once we knew that we were going to be at the hospital for more than a couple days, we decided that we wanted Max to be with us. After all, he was part of the family. Friends delivered him to Steve and Darlene's house in Fargo, where the kids and I dashed in and out to catch some sleep that harrowing week.

During the time we stayed with them, our routine at night was to come back to the house each evening. Darlene would draw me a bath, have candles burning near the tub, soft music playing, and low lighting to help me unwind before trying to sleep.

Now, my sister-in-law, who has a huge heart for animals, gave Max the royal dog treatment. One night, as I sat later than usual at the hospital with Randy, Darlene shot me a text and picture of what Max's life was like at their house. There he sat in their oversized Jacuzzi, wearing a medical scrub hat and basking in what appeared to be a spa experience. *You snooze … you lose*, she texted.

We all had a good laugh, a much-needed reprieve from the strain we endured at the hospital. Darlene understood. She got it. Dogs feel stress, too. Max needed a little extra TLC.

After Randy died, Max struggled. He seemed on edge, lost

in a daze, constantly looking for something … or *someone*. We assumed he was looking for Randy. We even talked to the funeral home about bringing Max to see him in the casket. Some might view this as little weird, I suppose, but Max was not himself. He was sad just like the rest of us. His behavior on his visit to the funeral home was strange. He sniffed around and near Randy but really didn't pay attention at all to his body.

We lifted him up to the casket and again Max had no interest in what he saw. He hunted around the room a little more and then it hit us, Randy's scent was gone. His body was there but *our* Randy, *his* Randy was not.

It was a real-world reminder to all of us that the soul he connected with was actually gone.

Because he remained unsettled and restless, several weeks later we drove him to the location where Randy had collapsed. Max didn't react.

During the following months, he moped, sad and alone. Several times he disappeared and ran away. After hours of searching, we would finally find him wandering the neighborhood. He just wasn't himself.

We were all at a loss. We even took Max to the vet, who checked for any physical problems. Pets, we learned, can suffer from grief. Max was mourning the loss of his best friend. I fully understood. I, too, had lost my best friend. Part of me was missing.

Before this, our routine had been to take daily walks, partially for the exercise but mostly because Max demanded it. It was really the only way to wear him out a bit from his puppy energy. Many days Max walked *me*. The jolly bounce in his step and his eagerness kept me going at a fast clip.

After Randy's death, the walks felt different, almost as though I had to drag Max along. He lost the bounce and kept a slow, somber pace. Obviously, he was not in the mood without his master.

After persistently walking him, I saw Max start to pull out of his sadness.

"The fresh air is doing us both some good," I told him. I quickened my pace and so did he.

When my friend Sandy offered to take him on runs, like he had enjoyed every day with Randy, it gave him a sense of normalcy. He was happy to discover a new running friend. Eventually, Max and I explored other routes with exciting new scents and untraveled paths. Like him, I was looking at the world a little differently. Together, we found our new groove.

Thirty-five

With my emotional life in pieces, I was on a trajectory to put myself back together.

Of course I already understood the importance of regular exercise, a balanced diet, and a sound sleep pattern as key components to living a healthy and long life. I read as much as I could about grief and clung to things I saw as helpful tools to living healthier. As the only parent to my three children, I now looked at life through a different lens, recognizing a new necessity: taking care of myself. For them.

My consistently tight chest made me feel like I was breathing through a teeny, tiny straw and couldn't get enough air. The pit in my stomach felt larger than ever. An eerie, overall unsettled and off feeling caused a bone-chilling fear of something undiagnosed. I suppose medical professionals would identify these odd symptoms as signs of anxiety and, medically, that might be correct. I summed them up as buried emotions begging to be released. Sometimes I excused myself from difficult situations to allow an opportunity for that to happen.

Fortunately for me, walking partners abounded. Max was always up for a brisk walk. Matthew joined us as his schedule allowed. My friend Diane and my sister Kathy walked with me when they could. Walks, talks, and tears—I was grateful for their listening ears. When I found myself alone, I slipped on headphones and played my favorite worship music. Sometimes I talked my way along the paths around town, buoying my spirits by releasing stress.

I could imagine Randy, a certified health nut, insisting that exercise equals sweating which equals burned calories. I chose to view myself as sweating from the inside out. By shedding tears, I was burning "grief calories." And that, I concluded, was a huge stride toward healing my heart and soul.

Feel-good endorphins after each walk became the only motivation I needed for a daily commitment. I burned off negative feelings and unwanted emotions that built up throughout the day. This natural, God-given antidepressant and getting outdoors stabilized my mental health. My mind cleared. I dwelled on the positive. The negatives were less domineering.

Prior to Randy's heart attack, I had encountered some health concerns that lead me down a life-changing path. At the recommendation of a co-worker, I had visited a doctor who specializes in natural healing to address my digestive issues. I began the process of changing my eating habits and learned important lessons about using food to heal my digestive tract.

Blood tests revealed intolerance to gluten and several other basic foods like green beans, asparagus, eggs, garlic, basil, and coffee. The virtues of consuming less refined sugar and unhealthy fat, fewer processed foods—while drinking plenty of water and not skipping meals—were givens. As I continued to eliminate the foods highlighted by allergy testing, I started to feel better. A great side effect was weight loss. Within several months of my new meal plan, I had dropped over forty pounds. By October, the loss was sixty-five pounds, life changing, to say the least. By the time Emily and Mitchell married a few months later, I had lost a total of eighty-seven pounds.

My recently acquired eating habits were a critical component to how I felt, how well I slept, and my overall emotional state. Motivation to eat right was directly related to the new responsibility I now shouldered. An unwelcome motivator, but a motivator nonetheless.

These healthy lifestyle changes necessitated revamping my mind, rhythm, and routine. Widowhood brought about some positive changes in my day-to-day life.

Sleep was an entirely different beast to conquer.

After wrestling through the nights following Randy's funeral, I visited my doctor who agreed that good sleep is critical to processing grief. He recommended an over-the-counter product or, alternatively, a prescription sleep aid. I chose the medication, excited at the prospect of finally sleeping through the night.

The first night I slept like a rock, deep and immovable. The problem was the morning-after effect. No matter how I tried, I woke in a fog, a feeling I did not like at all.

After discussing various options, the doctor advised cutting the pill in half. Even with a smaller dosage, I slept well. But in the morning, my kids teased, "You act like you're intoxicated!"

When I complained to a co-worker about the problem I'd encountered, she suggested I investigate essential oils. Stepping into unexplored territory, I phoned my friend Shawn who owned a physical therapy business.

"Serenity," she advised, "a unique blend of calming oils. A few drops of Serenity behind your ear about twenty minutes before bed will help relax your body naturally. Give it a try!"

Tentative about experimenting with something else, I reluctantly applied the drops that night. Relaxed, I slept the night through, just like Shawn claimed I would. Much to my surprise, I felt rested and energetic in the morning. I had found a fix.

From then on, I used a couple of drops behind my ears to ensure a sound sleep. Just like that, I was hooked on essential oils, a true believer!

My introduction to oils inspired me to experiment with them as a natural support for other ailments—emotional well-being, digestive and heart functions. My family received relief and benefits for many issues as we educated ourselves to use them. Even the dog benefitted when our veterinarian suggested we place lavender drops behind Max's ears to calm his anxiousness. Who would've thought!

Thirty-six

So many firsts to face that first year: Thanksgiving. Christmas. New Year's Eve. Valentine's Day. Easter. Father's Day. Our wedding anniversary. Independence Day. His birthday.

The dreaded the one-year anniversary of his death.

I worried as each occasion peered over the horizon. *How will it feel? How will I spend the day? Will I miss him so much that I won't be able to enjoy the day?*

As each important event surfaced, I struggled in the days leading up to it. I was out of sorts and felt like I needed to cry a lot. A huge stone settled in my stomach and wouldn't leave. I was on edge, impatient. My mind focused nowhere, wandering in a clouded mess. But when the actual day arrived, I was fine. And I survived them.

As our June wedding anniversary loomed, I knew it would be one of the hardest to endure.

It was *our* day, our wedding day. A day celebrated

exclusively between husband and wife.

Randy's absence was more than a gaping hole, leaving me with a happy memory and no one to share it. His absence was a particularly brutal reminder that I am no longer married to my soul mate, no longer part of a parenting team, no longer with my partner-for-life.

A wedding anniversary with no spouse is a huge finger pointing at loneliness. My aloneness. *I am single.*

Throughout the year, I learned that planning ahead for these key holidays is vital. Including extended family or close friends is equally important. I never let the day slip by unnoticed, but make sure I'm with others I trust and can be myself around.

I also experimented with journaling the occasions, a creative way to recognize the day in a blog-type post. It released my emotions, got them on paper and out of my mind.

With his birthday in August, we had typically grilled Randy's favorite meal of steak and potatoes and enjoyed his front-runner craft beers, mostly consisting of Summer Shandy. As the summer wore on, I decided early I wanted to celebrate my husband in a special way with close friends or family to "cheer" Randy on to another birthday in heaven.

We gathered at the lake. Jim made his famous barbeque ribs and we served the fixings to thirty of our family and close friends— who all sported new "Birthday—Run with Randy" tee-shirts.

So many feelings roiled inside me in advance of the event that, by the time the day finally arrived, it was not terrible at all. In fact, we had many laughs, shared stories and happy memories around the lake, and took an extra-long ride in the boat. I served birthday cake with candles and ended the night singing "Happy Birthday" to him.

There was no doubt I felt his absence, but I survived. The day after his birthday, I felt a burden lifted from my shoulders. I couldn't really explain the feeling but I wondered whether it was pure relief after the dread of the unknown feelings that might bombard me. Whatever the case may have been, planning a celebration certainly helped Randy's birthday go better than I expected.

Thirty-seven

From a young age, I suffered from homesickness or, as one doctor diagnosed, separation anxiety. Weeklong summer camps lasted only overnight. Sleepovers at the homes of friends ended early. During college, I came home every weekend because I couldn't bear being away longer. After growing up with such intense reactions, I thought I'd seen the worst of it.

When my daughter Emily attended Bible camp in third grade, she wrote letters home every day that she was gone. We received the stack of letters all at once, on the same day we were headed to bring her home.

The first letter read: *"COME* and *GET* me *NOW*! Get in the car *IMMEDIATELY*. I want to come home NOW."

The next letter was a little less frantic, and her homesickness receded as we read each succeeding letter. In fact, her change of heart was a complete one-eighty by the time we opened the final envelope.

"DON'T come and *GET* me for another *WEEK*! I'm having too much fun."

If you ever went away to camp as a kid you might be acquainted with the feeling of homesickness, the longing in your chest. You miss your bed, your family, your mom's cooking, the very *smell* of your house. There's a hollow space in your stomach that is never filled … until you get home.

Widowhood feels like the worst kind of summer camp experience *ever.* It is like being homesick … with one huge difference: Going home doesn't ease or erase the feeling—because you never really get to go home.

You made your home *in another person* and, when he's gone, so is your sense of home. No one and no thing really fills that hollow spot in your stomach. No one can bring him back. And no one or no thing can take you back home.

Confirmation of this feeling came as I was having dinner one night with my neighbor Rena who had recently lost her husband.

"It's like I'm homesick," she said, "only I can't go home."

I nodded in agreement. Being homesick yet nothing could fix it or make it better.

MercyMe was one of Randy's favorite Christian bands. In fact, we included their song, "I Can Only Imagine" at his funeral. One day, I encountered their song, "Homesick."

> *You're in a better place,*
> *I've heard a thousand times*
> *And at least a thousand times*
> *I've rejoiced for you*
> *But the reason why I'm broken,*
> *the reason why I cry*
> *Is how long must I wait to be with you.*

As I listened to the lyrics define the longings of my heart, tears flowed.

Always known as a glass-half-full person, I recognized how widowhood caused me to be more of a realist. I wanted God to bring Randy home NOW. I knew it couldn't happen; I knew it wouldn't happen. I also knew God understood and was helping me cope. He strengthened me.

Over time, much like Emily's camp letters, I noticed the homesickness slipping away. I, too, began to find joy. I was involved and busy. The crippling yearning in my chest was no longer front and center in my mind. I was learning to live with the ache. Just as Mary had "…treasured up all these things and pondered them in her heart," (Luke 2:19 NIV), I cherished every reminder of my loved one's profound impact on my life. I learned to replace the loneliness with a feeling of deep gratitude for my time with Randy, a man worth being homesick for.

Thirty-eight

The weeks leading up to the one-year anniversary of
Randy's death were much like people had warned me, with all the
symptoms they had listed. Anxiousness. Short-fused temperament.
Homesickness, stronger than previous months. An ache in my
heart that had not been there for a while. November 1 landed on
a Sunday, so spending the weekend with family in Minneapolis
seemed like an obvious way to commemorate the red-letter day.

The cross-country team had reached out weeks prior,
offering to do another Run with Randy, which we scheduled for the
one-year anniversary of his collapse on October 26. I was touched
and honored that they wanted to keep his memory alive with an
additional run.

Late October can be a wild card for Minnesota weather,
but we went ahead with the race despite cold temperatures and a
light snow. The police escorted our runners the entire way, from the
location of Randy's collapse to Breckenridge High. Friends, family,

and the community at large joined us at the finish line, where we told more Randy stories. Pastor Mark, Randy's assistant cross-country coach and friend, led the group in prayer as we released helium balloons—our way to let the world know we were honoring the life of a wonderful man.

We ended the morning in routine fashion over our favorite protein shakes with our friends at Lovin' Nutrition. The nutrition club employees wore their Run with Randy tee-shirts and donated a portion of their sales to the Run with Randy Memorial.

A few days later, Matthew and Marcia accompanied me to Minneapolis to support my niece, Annie, in her college performance of "Phantom of the Opera." We met up with Emily, my sister Kathy's family, and my mom, who surprised us all when she arrived from her winter home in Estero, Florida. Of course, the weekend involved some tears and sadness as we spoke of the events of the prior years. But joy infused us as we reminisced about Randy, even wondering what he might be doing that day to celebrate his heavenly birthday.

Randy's brother Steven capped the day by posting a tribute on Facebook that left me in awe of another God moment.

Steve Berndt
November 1, 2015 · 👥

I worked a 12 hour shift in the OR at Sanford today. I've been thinking about my brother Randy a lot. He died here in OR 11 one year ago today. Darlene and I were among a small group of family members with him in the OR waiting for his heart to stop after discontinuing life support. At one point Jana leaned close to his face and softly said, "It's alright, you can go now. We're gonna miss you, but we'll be OK." I don't know whether he could hear or process her words, but after that a single tear rolled out of the corner of his eye, and his kind, generous, loving, humble heart stopped. It was 9:05 AM, November 1, 2014.

In a surreal twist of fate, I was in OR 11 at 9:05 this morning, participating in the briefing prior to another organ recovery case. The circumstances were different, but the big picture was the same. One family is grieving while in other hospitals in other cities other families are rejoicing because their loved ones are getting new life. Randy would be smiling about that.

What were the odds of Steven being in the same OR room—at the exact time he was one year ago? Coincidence? I think not. Randy managed to show up again, a reminder that he was with us in spirit.

The anniversary came … and went. Much less painful than I had anticipated. Once again, the most difficult part was the dread and worry leading up to that day. We had survived a full year without Randy at our side. He would be proud!

Year Two

UNTANGLING

Thirty-nine

Although books and advice-givers had done their best to prepare me for The Year of Firsts, there was scant forewarning of what I might face beyond those difficult twelve months. As I began to encounter annual events, holidays, and milestones for the second time around, I realized I had plunged into another year without Randy. It stung. A sharp bee sting that left a pain nothing could ease.

My people were still very much present for me with check-in texts and hot meals and friendship. A lot of things that helped comfort me earlier, however, weren't what I found myself wanting now. There was no way for others to fulfill needs that I was still defining.

I had cowered behind the safety net of family and close friends, but when the calendar flipped to 2016, my internal calendar reminded me that I had some inside work to do. As text messages slowed and invitations to dinner tapered, anxiety crept in. Outwardly I wore a survivor's face while my insides were in shambles.

I struggled against loneliness, a battle between heart and mind that I had to fight by myself. I couldn't pass off my grief like a basketball to another player. This wasn't a team sport. All I could do was dribble and shoot.

Trying to piece together the past in order to move forward, I discovered blank spots—missing days or events. It was as though my memory was washed away by my sorrow. The kids would talk about an event or something we did and I had no recollection of the occasion. If we hadn't had photographs to prove otherwise, I would have sworn I wasn't present.

This was also true of everyday routines; the simplest of things slipped my mind.

Matthew, still living at home, spent a lot of time with me. We had numerous conversations about recent events or happenings that couldn't jog my memory, even a bit. At first, I was convinced he was making things up or playing tricks. Then I worried. Was it possible I was losing my mind?

One night over dinner, he mentioned my red Buick Enclave.

"What red Enclave?" I countered. "I never had a red Enclave. It was black."

We argued back and forth—until he pulled out his cellphone and scrolled to a picture of the Buick sitting in my parking spot, in our garage. I was stunned.

"You traded your black one in early 2015," he chided.

Still, I couldn't pull up the occasion. Even after more discussion, I never pieced it together. Why was my memory so incredibly poor?

Visiting with Dr. Halvorson, my primary physician, I recapped specific instances and expressed my concern about my failed power of recollection. He assured me that this was normal, simply my brain's way of protecting me from overload during a time of mourning. I needed to give myself grace during these moments. Easier to write than to understand and believe.

Forty

During all the years I was married to Randy, I was part of an incredible team and never had to face anything without my partner at my side. Now I was quickly discovering that God didn't create us to do life alone. Some tasks were too overwhelming for me to handle without my husband.

One fall day, I looked out the door at all the leaves on the lawn and knew I should tackle the raking. *This will be a great way to clean up the yard and enjoy the fall air*, I thought. What a sense of accomplishment I would feel by doing the task, a small victory to celebrate.

Matthew agreed to help his mom rake all the leaves that had collected over the previous few weeks and mow the lawn hiding somewhere underneath them all. To say it was a daunting task would be an immense understatement. We filled dozens of bags as we raked and gathered the roughage—much more draining than the emotional capacity I had that day.

Overcome with frustration, I stomped to the side of the house with tears in my eyes and began to silently grumble to Randy.

"Why did you do this to me? How dare you leave me on this earth alone—with this entire yard to care for? There's no way you or God expects me to rake all these on my own!"

After a few minutes, I pulled myself together as best I could and returned to the front yard. It was as though Randy had heard my complaints and answered. Our neighbor Terry came riding over on his lawn tractor outfitted with a bagger.

My heart swelled in relief. God was in the details!

Within a short amount of time, much quicker than Matthew and I would have been able to handle it, the lawn was mowed, cleaned up, and bags hauled to the composting site.

Terry was such a blessing to us that day. Thank goodness, I hadn't followed my first instinct to reject his offer and worry that it inconvenienced him or was too much to expect or that I was copping out or …I'd probably still be trying to do all the work myself.

I had to learn to humble myself, ask for, and accept help from others. Twice the blessings: them in the giving, me in the receiving.

Forty-one

Emily, who always had a love of writing, grieved by starting a blog site to host her thoughts and reflections. For her, blogging was a way to release hostile, dangerous emotions. Her anxiety and depression didn't seem so big and scary once it was out of her mind and on the page of her journal. I believe she would say journaling saved her life on more than one occasion.

She got me started on my own blog site, which allowed me to share my thoughts with loved ones. As I wrote my journey, I found a measure of joy as I discovered the ways God came through for us.

I'd always been intrigued by words. In the beginning journaling was hard, at times overwhelming. I started thinking about what I wanted to release from my mind. As soon as I opened the floodgates, a steady stream of all of these thoughts and emotions I just had to get out.

There were also days when I wanted so badly to express

myself, but as much as I tried, the words wouldn't come. Writing, I learned, is a creative and healing process I couldn't force. Words flow when the time is right and my mind is willing to release and process them.

Blogging reintroduced me to the healing power offered by writing. A wonderful gift that helped my mind process my broken heart, writing allowed me to capture my whirling thoughts and pin them down where I could make sense of them. Some days I spewed burdensome, toxic emotions. Tension and anxiety seeped from my body with each new paragraph. The more I blogged, the more I could be fully present.

In addition, my intimate circle of friends and reading audience seemed to appreciate the updates. So many had become invested in our story and wanted to know how we were doing. This was their way of staying connected without infringing on our privacy.

As I've discovered, journaling and storytelling can take many different art forms: written words, photography, video, music, sewing, jewelry, and other creative methods.

Picture gathering has always been a hobby of mine, and for years I have been taking and collecting pictures from every possible angle. I developed a storytelling photographic style. Not mere portraits, but pictures to relive our family vacations and daily routines.

Searching for photos to use at Randy's funeral, we scrolled through 125,000 images on my computer! Bless my sister's heart for all her hard work in putting them together—and also for talking me out of printing and framing all 125,000. They are amazing keepsakes, more precious with each passing year.

I found ways to preserve the memories of Randy and our years together: I journaled memories into photo books, a priceless keepsake. Telling Randy's life in words and pictures was healing and fulfilling.

Another keepsake opportunity arose when my friend Julie

offered to make the kids and me four tee-shirt quilts from Randy's clothing. I gifted the quilts to them as we moved out of our Maple Street home, leaving our memories of that house behind. With their dad's scent still on them, the quilts felt like Randy's arms wrapped around us.

Excited to discover other creative ideas, I hired a seamstress to make toss pillows out of his dress shirts. Another co-worker, Sharon, had a friend style warm winter mittens from his sweaters. Preserving a few of Randy's belongings was a unique way to remember his life and how much he meant to us. The mementos made heart-warming Christmas gifts for Randy's siblings, nieces, nephews, and close friends.

Forty-two

The world said, *Keep going!* But my grieving heart kept saying, *Slow down.*

Activities, friends, events hurtled by as I found myself saying I need to step back and breathe deeply.

Linda Ellis's poem, "The Dash," impacted and supported my intuition. Our days are numbered, she wrote. We will die. Birth-death, that's our life. The question becomes: When your family puts your name and dates on your tombstone, what really matters is the dash between those numbers represents our life spent on earth. "…and now only those who loved them know what that little line is worth."

How am I spending my dash? I wondered.

It's so easy to overcommit until you're run ragged. Attending, committing, serving, volunteering, leading …It was a Berndt family trait, a curse. We ran and ran just to stay involved and active.

Demands on my time and energy took a physical and emotional demand on me. My fulltime job at the bank, where I managed projects, people, and client interactions, required my focused attention and more energy than ever before now that my mind juggled other demanding thoughts. My community involvement was at a peak in my career: I chaired several boards that bid for more of my mind and time. Church commitments clamored more for a share of me, too. I was the regular pianist, month after month, planning worship, practicing with other musicians, playing for worship, going home and starting over again for the next week. Something had to give. My body and mind could not keep up with those around me and I knew, *I knew* I needed to slow down, simplify, give my heart a chance to heal. Dealing with grief and the motivation to move through this journey in a healthy way was now a primary focus.

What would God have me do?

But those who hope in the Lord will renew their strength. They will soar on wings like eagles; they will run and not grow weary, they will walk and not be faint. (Isaiah 40:31)

The Eagle Brook Church daily app on my phone includes a daily devotional along with weekly messages from Pastors Bob and Jason. Their profound "Seven Words That Will Change Your Life" series resonated with me. Seven words? I could manage seven words.

Yes. No. Thanks. Enough. Sorry. Help. Wow. These seven words were life-changing.

"No" and "enough" had a huge impact as I considered my troubled heart, soul, and mind. It seemed almost too obvious and simple.

Enough, Jana! I told myself. *You need to say "no" to all the busyness in your life and "yes" to things that really matter.*

It was time to reevaluate my life and the direction I was

going, to isolate those things that really mattered.
I needed to make sure my heart was right with God. I
needed to be certain I was devoting enough time to those most
important things. The message on the simple word "enough" helped
frame my definition of contentment.

I had spent much of my life wanting to plunge into The
Next Big Thing. The problem was that wishing and wanting got
in the way of enjoying the here and now. I got tricked into the
mentality of *when this happens, then it will all be better.* I focused
on what I could attain, *when I get this, my life will be much richer,
fuller.* These kinds of thoughts can go on and on. Before I know it, I
can get stuck in a place of always wanting more and more, like it's
just never enough.

The sermon inspired me to journal, mostly ideas on how
to simplify. I needed to give up some habits and those committees
or that activities no longer were meaningful in order to incorporate
more of what brings me joy.

I considered what was important to me. These are the things
I listed: Make more time for walks; plan healthier meals; arrange for
dinners or lunches with close friends; continue to keep family as my
number one.

Next, I considered what I needed to eliminate. That list was
easy: Resign from a few committees that no longer really needed
my talent; retire from being the full-time "weekend" musician;
refuse meaningless invitations; resist pleas to get involved in "the
next best thing for our community."

This was all easier written than practiced, but I did see
my schedule slowing. In addition to letting go of some of the
external commitments in my life, I decided to be more aware of
the conversations or "problems" I took on. Listening to others'
drama drained me. This was a good time to remove myself from the
frivolous chatter and involvement that overshadowed my needs.

Enjoying the here and now—being content with where God
put me—seemed to be the key to living a balanced, well-adjusted

life in my new norm.

That first summer, I spent many nights in the garden pulling weeds, deadheading flowers, simply soaking in God's nature. Birds trilled. Fresh air cooled my arms. Blossoms scented the yard. I looked around the soothing stillness.

This, I decided, *is a good example of slowing down.*

Forty-three

The approaching spring gave me a sense of renewal. Temperatures softened as we climbed out of the deep freeze. Walks with Max were a little more tolerable and my closet would soon fill with bright colors again. So, why did I feel … unsettled? I had survived one full year but plunged into the second plagued by a permanent cloud over my head. My sleep patterns were interrupted. My tears came too easily. My composure was fragile.

Over our favorite health shakes, I shared my concerns with Marcia.

She toyed with her straw a bit before looking directly into my eyes. "Jana, maybe it's time to seek some outside help. Have you considered it?"

Marcia had stuck to my side through the lows of the past many months. Her suggestion to add a new voice gave me pause. Reservations surfaced. It had been hard enough to juggle and interpret all the well-meaning comments and questions that seemed to be part of widowhood. I couldn't imagine reliving it all with strangers. I shuddered at the thought.

"At least promise me you'll consider it?" Marcia urged.

After mulling it over and praying about it, I mustered my courage. I phoned Jeanne, the grief-care counselor at the funeral home. Months earlier when she suggested a grief class, I had dismissed the idea and said I was doing well. My support of family and friends was strong. Now, I reluctantly admitted I needed help. She registered me in their upcoming session along with five other widows of varying ages and circumstances. We attended weekly meetings to share and explore our individual sorrows as a grief community.

At first I felt awkward. Most of the women were much further along in their life than I was. I considered myself a young widow by comparison and was hesitant to think I could benefit from their perspectives. However, when I opened myself to their stories I realized how much I could learn from others walking a similar road. Difficult though it was, the experience helped me through my struggle.

One of the more profound lessons it taught me was that age is not a factor in the depth and breadth of grief. Everyone travels a similar path, regardless of life stage or experience.

I had promised myself, my family, and especially my kids I would do whatever it took to make sure I was mourning in a healthy way. I didn't want to leave any stone unturned. I did not want to live with regret about my experiences in the grieving process, anything that might eventually threaten my progress toward healing. I needed a fresh, clean start to discover my new norm and leave behind some of the hurt and pain that lingered in my heart. I owed this to my three kids, to Randy … to me.

The book study and group discussion guides gave us the tools to teach, support, and encourage each other. Hearing so many of my private thoughts and feelings put into words through others' stories dulled the loneliness I sometimes felt. I discovered a level of comfort as I shared this experience with other women.

At one point, we were asked to make a timeline of major events, both the good and the bad, calling attention to the highs and lows in our lives, exposing anything left unsettled, hanging. With Randy gone, I had no other way to reconcile those buried feelings.

This paved the way for the final step of the course ... handwritten "goodbye" letters. I can't sugarcoat it. It was a downright ugly, painful process.

For several weeks I wrote, erased, and mustered words I wanted to say to Randy. I did *not* want to say goodbye, and I certainly did not want to put it in writing. Something about putting it on paper meant that it truly was over. Done. Real. Final.

If I write it down, my marriage will be dead and Randy will be out of my life.

Tears flowed and splattered as I wrote.

The day arrived when we were asked to read our letters aloud. Raw emotion, gritty sorrow, and palpable apprehension swirled around the room, so thick I couldn't breathe. I wanted to go home and hide under my covers. Did the other widows encounter the same gut-wrenching anxiety in the pits of their stomachs? Would I be able to read through my strangled throat?

I panicked, feeling unprepared. Unwilling. Although I practiced at home a few times, I could never make it through without breaking down. In fact, I couldn't even make it through the first few paragraphs before I'd have to take a time-out to sob and get myself under control.

From somewhere, I found the courage to take my turn.

March 21, 2016

Dear Randy,

I can't believe I'm sitting here at fifty-four years old, writing a "goodbye" letter to you. This is not what we had planned for our life together and it's unbelievable that it's come to this. But as I continue to move forward in this life without you by my side, I am reminded of some things that have been left unsaid or are on my heart that I want to share with you now.

Randy, I want you to know that every day I continue to pray and thank God that I found you and that I got to marry my best friend on June 21, 1986. I want you to know that I loved our time together, our three beautiful children, and the many trips we took, especially our tenth anniversary trip to San Francisco when I was pregnant with Matthew. It was like a second honeymoon for us.

Randy, I want you to know that I am forever grateful that Mitchell included us in his proposal to Emily. Seeing you so excited and placing that ring on the sandcastle is an image I will never forget. We only have a couple of hundred pictures to prove it. :) The engagement party and bridal shower in August were Divine Intervention. You making the "Father of the Bride" speech nine months before the wedding was priceless. Who could ever know?

The following months were all a preparation of your death in November starting with our new health kick. You were my biggest cheerleader in helping me meet my weight loss and exercise goal. I loved our walks and talks. I will always remember when we bought our dream home. It was hard to wait, thinking it would be six months before we could move in. But God knew we needed that time before we left our Maple Street home with all your stuff—but not you. I will always remember our walk around the block one night, our routine. This particular night we talked about life as it was shortly after your dad had passed away. I remember saying, "I don't know what I would ever do if something happened to you." I remember you saying you would want me to find someone to move on with. What a gift.

Randy I want you to know that your final gift of organ donation was the ultimate gift and so fitting for you and your legacy. Sixty-two families were affected by your generous gift of life and I am so proud of you and the wonderful husband and father you have been to our family.

Randy I want you to know that I am proud to be your wife and a part of me will be always be with you. As I move forward, I take with me many happy memories of our life together. I love and miss you deeply Randy. Until we are together, forever—goodbye, Randy Berndt.

While this is just a fraction of the goodbye note I painstakingly prepared, I read my letter in its entirety to the class. Between the tears and breakdowns, I sensed a measure of healing in my heart. Maybe that was the point of this whole exercise. To exercise my recovery muscle.

Regardless of how ugly it was, once it was all over, I had said goodbye to Randy.

I had forgiven him for things that were undone or unfinished. I had released unsettled feelings within myself. And I couldn't deny it felt good. I had desperately needed to let go of intense and sometimes not-so-pretty emotions.

The process of writing and reading the letter out loud made it a healing experience. It didn't erase lingering traces of sadness and longing, but the class allowed me to loosen my grip on the past, to resolve unfinished business, to reveal hidden fears and sorrows I had not yet faced.

Forty-four

My faith and my prayer life had been present before Randy's death. We attended church on a regular basis. We prayed before meals and before bedtime. We read devotionals from time to time. I was involved in church and played piano for almost thirty years, serving as co-director of music for just over twenty years.

From my point of view, I was a strong Christian with a real faith. I never really had faced a situation where my only way to survive was to put my entire trust in Him. But now it was time to put my professed faith to the test and see how strong my roots and beliefs really were. I had to let God take charge of my life.

I felt the Lord nudging me to read more scripture, read more books, and make sure to start and end every day in prayer with Him. I felt the truth of the scripture, "God is close to the brokenhearted" because I felt Him drawing me closer through my experience of grief. As I drew closer to Him, I felt His presence, guidance, and peace in my life grow stronger. I knew that each leap of faith I took only brought me to know God more and more.

I was also conscious of the many people, onlookers, closely watching us. I felt them searching for a deeper meaning and knew my reaction and response to this tragedy—the very way it defined my faith—mattered more than ever. I could feel the importance of the testimony my story could be for others seeking answers.

It was like a test. A really big test.

During Randy's final hours, I stood in the hospital hallway talking to my friend John, mere minutes before making the decision to remove life supports. I confided my deep fear of facing a future without Randy.

"Jana, you have more faith than anyone else I know," he reassured me. "You can do this life without Randy. It will be sad and even pretty hard, but you can do it. You have a deep faith."

As hard as it's been, and as much as I didn't want any of this, my widowhood has redefined my faith in ways I never thought possible. I've grown and discovered more about the Lord than I knew there was to discover.

Forty-five

One of the strange things I had wanted to do while I sat with Randy in ICU was to read. I needed to get my hands on anything and everything that would help me understand what he was going through. I felt an intense need to somehow become as knowledgeable as the brain surgeon and neurologist in a matter of hours. Unrealistic, I know. Yet it felt like the more I knew, the better equipped I might be to handle the decisions ahead of me.

This need to read and desire to increase my knowledge continued into the months following his death. The more I could read and learn about what others had experienced, the better prepared I would be for whatever was ahead of me.

I devoured the materials on grief provided by the hospital and funeral home. I scoured the Internet for resources. I accepted books and articles from others who had traveled a similar path. Knowledge was my friend, my armor.

My earlier worry and anxiety seemed to stem from the

unknown. *Will I be okay? Will I be able to endure this tragedy?*

Interestingly, reading was never my forte. I never cared to read. It didn't interest me. In fact, during elementary and middle school, reading was a challenge rather than a strength as it is for many students.

Now I found myself challenged by the breadth and depth—and amount—of information I discovered. There was so much of it, mostly from a perspective and knowledge level impossible for me to relate to or apply to myself.

Being in the deepest part of my grief, I realized my brain was not capable of reading most of this technically written material. What I really needed was something easy to absorb, something practical for the specific stages of my life.

The few articles and books that resonated with me, I read and re-read several times, the pages dog-eared and worn from the hours I spent learning and trying to apply.

The books prepared me for the standardized stages of grief: denial, anger, bargaining, depression, acceptance. The more I read the more I wanted to beat the odds and not fall into the typical stages. How could everyone who has a loss feel the same emotion? Wasn't that too much like textbook jargon?

Shock, sadness, fear, worry, resilience, and peace. Those were the descriptive words I would choose to describe my grief. Similar, yet not the cookie cutter approach the books cited.

Shock or disbelief? I had multiple situations when I heard Randy's voice or expected him to walk in through the back door. I struggled to grasp the reality of him not being present.

Time and time again I stood before the fireplace mantel to study the large canvas photograph of our family, smiling and complete. I still couldn't wrap my mind around the reality that he was gone. I stared at the picture, forcing myself to believe he was no longer with us. It simply didn't feel real.

When the initial shock passed, a profound sadness took its place. I moved from operating on autopilot to a sinking state of despair. An achy feeling that made me hurt everywhere—especially in my heart. Maybe it *is* possible to have a broken heart.

My bottomless sadness at Randy's absence seemed to emphasize the utter loneliness of being single.

Our marriage was a friendship based on mutual respect, love for God, and love for our family. We treasured our time together and rarely had a disagreement. This is not to say we were perfect, but we held dear our many years of love and the memories we'd made throughout our marriage.

I found myself reassuring friends and family, "I have no regrets."

And I truly didn't. Our relationship was strong with no unresolved issues or lingering misgivings. My only disappointment? That we didn't get more time together.

I simply missed him. I missed our talks, our walks, the hours we carved out for each other.

Shortly after his death, I bought a sign for my bathroom: *If I had to do my life all over again, I'd find you sooner so I could love you longer.*

Every morning my eyes searched out the words and I would nod, thinking how true it was. I wanted more of him. His days were cut short; so was our time together.

Forty-six

Randy's death cast a cloud on my days, so when the calendar flipped to March, I surprised myself by the burst of laughter that erupted when I noticed the date: March 14 or, in my husband's world, International Pi Day. For him it was a day for an all-out, geeky celebration. And Randy ranked highest among the high of avid math geeks.

He always began the morning by donning his Pi Day shirt—amply accessorized with a Pi formula necktie and Pi socks. Oh, yeah, the middle schoolers saw him coming from a distance.

His students especially looked forward to class that day, knowing it would be filled with funky contests, quirky quizzes, and dazzling fun facts. Prizes, bestowed liberally, included Little Debbie pies for those who could recite, from memory, at least ten digits of the infinite string of numbers: 3.141592653….

Pi Day validated Randy's purpose as a teacher, a career that gave him ample satisfaction.

Grinning from ear to ear, I made certain we continued the tradition by gathering to remember his laughter, his pride in his students, his utter joy in teaching and, of course, to eat pie!

Consequently, I was especially touched that our community and distant loved ones wanted to make certain we left a mark of Randy's legacy in more significant ways during 2016.

LifeSource invited us to the Twin Cities for an annual recognition event for donor families. Several dignitaries made remarks aimed at those of us still grieving and wanting to keep our loved ones' memories alive. Though the comments were rewarding and healing, they conjured still-tender memories of my husband's last week of life.

After one of them related Randy's story, we were asked to approach the stage for his "medal of honor." Reluctantly, I dragged myself to the front, followed by Tyler, Matthew, Marcia, and Kathy.

Why in the world did you put yourself in this position? What ever made you accept this invitation?

We hugged the presenters, accepted the medal and made our way back to our seats. Simultaneously overcome with pride and sadness, I wrestled with thoughts of what it had meant for Randy to be an organ donor. Randy died; his organ recipients reclaimed their lives. Our family lost Randy; other families won.

It's not a matter of win or lose, came the reconciling thought. Randy collapsed, died, and had, fortunately, pre-orchestrated his end-of-life wishes to include transplants. He saw that his earthly body was used up, spent, maxed.

No, this was not a win/lose scenario—this was life lived to its fullest.

In April, National Organ Donation Month, Matthew and I were invited to Sanford Hospital's LifeSource recognition program. My invitation included the opportunity to tell *our* story of Randy, my first public attempt to speak on behalf of our family and tell others about my wonderful husband.

Walking into Sanford Hospital for the first since Randy's

death was an out-of-body experience. I immediately regretted my decision to attend and wanted nothing more than to turn around and go home—especially seeing that the ceremony was being held in the lounge where we camped during Randy's hospital stay. As I approached the garden, my eyes swept upward and blurred. The Donate Life flag fluttered. My breath caught.

What was I thinking? I'm not strong enough for this!

I should have agreed to attend but not speak, let Steven speak on our behalf.

The chaplain opened the ceremony. "Sunflowers do an amazing sun-following trick," she began, "a trick that makes these plants seem to possess some mystical powers."

I didn't quite make the connection between this "mystical" power and organ donation, but that I was standing in the crowd, waiting my turn to speak on a topic dear and deep, was truly mystical and eerie.

As staff and volunteers placed golden flowers, one by one, in the vase on the table, I saw the analogy as a sign. They couldn't have known that the summer I met Randy he worked in the sunflower industry, where he would spend fifteen years. A peace settled over me and gave me courage.

With Matthew at my side and my mother-in-law and Marcia silently cheering me on from the audience, I did it. I talked about my husband, his death, his gift of life, and our survival of it all. Telling our story was hard, but there was healing in relating everything publicly.

During the afternoon, I met an organ recipient who received a heart and lung transplant eleven years earlier and had been trying to connect with her organ donor's family. She hadn't yet received a response. Because we had not heard anything from Randy's recipients, her efforts reassured me. Understanding I might never connect with any of them, I decided on the spot to keep praying for them. But I wouldn't give up hoping.

A dream materialized in my heart: *Someday, we will Run*

with Randy—joined by the man who received Randy's right lung.

When May arrived, Tyler challenged our family to a fitness outing in preparation for the annual Fargo Marathon. Running was a pipe dream for me, an impossibility.

"Not so quick to judge, Mom," Tyler said. "You can do it!"

When I mentioned the goal to others, I chuckled at their reactions.

"Are you running the full or the half marathon?" many asked.

My sister, who quickly tired of their mundane rhetoric, crafted her own response. "We're doing the full 5K," she would say with a serious face, and watch for their startled reactions.

For Kathy and me, this 5K was more than a marathon. Sporting our Run with Randy tee-shirts, we wound our way around the campus of North Dakota State University, Randy's alma mater. Fantasizing about his college days and how he may have spent his time as an NDSU Bison, we raced and walked, with perseverance— crossing the finish line in a time faster than I had clocked since beginning my fitness routine.

The participation medals we all received were inscribed: "Let us run with perseverance the race that is marked out of us." (Hebrews 12:1-2 NIV) Not by chance, this was the verse we had adopted and spoken at Randy's funeral and had imprinted on more than 1,000 tee-shirts. Now on the medal of our family challenge, this strong message reminded us that Randy was with us. The run marked another milestone in our effort to move forward in our life without his physical presence.

Tyler made the family proud the following day when he ran the half marathon and received a second medal with the Hebrews insignia. Watching him cross the finish line, I lost myself in the memory of a few short years prior when I cheered him and his dad across the same finish line.

It had been Tyler's senior year of college and he was nursing a leg injury. Even so, he and Randy had trained over the winter months and, in the end, decided to run the half marathon. A father-son duo. Faster than his fifty-one-year-old father, Tyler hung back, pushing Randy to a faster finish. The last mile was tense for them both. Neck-in-neck, the partners crossed the line in 1:44, making their goal of under 1:45. Emily and Matthew held up their "Cheer!" signs and I photographed the moment. We etched this run in our minds forever.

Now here I was in Fargo, watching Tyler cross the finish line again. Another bittersweet moment.

Spring also brought multiple opportunities to speak publicly about Randy.

On one occasion, we bestowed the second annual Run with Randy award to a graduating eighth grader who had demonstrated many of Randy's honorable characteristics. Carson Hought joined the prior year's recipient, Nolan Lemna. He was chosen by teachers and administrators based on his work ethic, compassion, and other attributes which set him apart in Breckenridge schools. After opening comments and recognitions, Principal Erickson turned the microphone over to me.

I started my presentation by sharing stories about my husband. This was the last class to have had Mr. Berndt as their math teacher, something special to hold on to. My comments, heartfelt and a tad emotional, were abruptly interrupted by the loudspeaker.

Gail, the school secretary, announced, "The senior class of 2016 is taking their final stroll through the elementary and middle school." Students were asked to line the hallways and greet the seniors as they passed by.

What timing.

Principal Erickson suggested I finish my speech and go forward with the award. Agreeably, I began … when the loudspeaker belted out "Humble and Kind," a Tim McGraw song.

I took it as another sign: Randy was taking charge, preventing me from going on and on about how wonderful he was and how these kids should be more like him. He preferred that Carson receive the award and listen to the song.

I had to agree. The lyrics were more fitting than what I planned to say. Carson was considerate, "humble and kind." Just like Randy.

Forty-seven

Spring swiftly segued into a much-needed summer and the normality of weekend family time at the lake.

Besides the addition of our family cabin, Buck Saw Lodge, one of the best changes came when our family discovered Calvary at the Lake—an outdoor worship experience in Douglas County. The unique church setting overlooks beautiful Lake Carlos, one of Minnesota's many breathtaking lakes, and provides a vibrant worship time and surreal atmosphere.

One of Pastor Hans's messages struck a resounding chord with me and prompted an inspiring and reflective discussion around the topic of our stuff. Our treasures. The things into which we pour our time, energy, and resources. And our heart follows suit.

I often thought about all of Randy's stuff, how it really didn't matter how much or how little he had, and how it didn't matter how much stress I put into it. He didn't take one single thing with him when he died. I'd heard many funeral sermons iterate,

"There's never been a hearse pulling a trailer behind it." My take-away from the pastor's lesson, combined with my personal grief lessons, was profound: just like Randy, I couldn't take anything with me.

Our stuff is just our stuff, only found on earth. In heaven, we will have all we need, and the small stuff we worry about on earth really isn't important.

My relationships, my emotional and spiritual well-being were what really mattered.

When I looked at my calendar and how I spent my time, when I assessed my bank account and where my money went, did they align with the things I valued most? Was I spending my time, energy, and resources on the big things that mattered most? Or was I sweating the small stuff?

Even though the move had encouraged purging and reassigning many of Randy's possessions, many boxes of his clothing and artifacts had made their way to Crescent Drive. After Pastor Hans's sermon opened my eyes, I worked my way through them—taking time to reminisce, rub a sweater against my cheek, swipe at the moisture gathering in my eyes—and sorted items for donation. My strength to deal with his clothing came in waves and it took months to really make any sort of progress. But the must-keep pile shrank drastically and Goodwill was the benefactor of some really nice and fashionable clothing.

RANDY'S 8TH BIRTHDAY ON THE FAMILY FARM IN
BRECKENRIDGE MN, 1970. PICTURED: GARY, STEVEN,
KEITH AND AMY.

RANDY'S SCHOOL PHOTO TAKEN MERE
WEEKS BEFORE HIS DEATH IN 2014.

JANA AND RANDY BERNDT, AT THE FIRST
PRESBYTERIAN CHURCH IN CROOKSTON MN,
JUNE 21, 1986.

LAST PHOTO TAKEN OF JANA AND
RANDY AS A COUPLE, MOUNT CARMEL,
ALEXANDRIA MN, OCTOBER 2014.

TYLER AND RANDY AT THE FARGO
HALF MARATHON, SPRING 2012.

MATTHEW AND HIS DAD AT THEIR 5K
WALK/RUN THE DAY BEFORE RANDY'S
COLLAPSE ON OCTOBER 24, 2014.

EMILY AND HER DAD REVELING IN A BELOVED
BOAT RIDE, JULY 4, 2013.

ALWAYS READY FOR
ADVENTURE, RANDY ON *HIS
LARSON*, AIMED TOWARD RAINY
LAKE, LAKE OF THE WOODS,
CANADA, AUGUST 2007.

THE RANDY BERNDT FAMILY'S LAST GROUP PHOTO TAKEN AT THE FUNERAL OF RANDY'S DAD, OCTOBER 5, 2014.

RUN WITH RANDY LOGO DESIGNED FOR THE FIRST RWR RACE, BY NIECE AND NEPHEW, CAYLA AND JARED, NOVEMBER 2014.

FLAG RAISING CEREMONY TO SIGNIFY THE START OF THE ORGAN TRANSPLANT PROCESS FOR RANDY'S DONATION, OCTOBER 2014.

FIRST CHRISTMAS WITHOUT RANDY, AT FORT MYERS BEACH FL, 2014.

TYLER, EMILY AND MATTHEW CHEERING ON THEIR DAD, RANDY, AT THE FARGO MARATHON, MAY 2009.

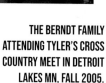

THE BERNDT FAMILY ATTENDING TYLER'S CROSS COUNTRY MEET IN DETROIT LAKES MN, FALL 2005.

EMILY AND MITCHELL'S WEDDING, AT MOUNT CARMEL, ALEXANDRIA MN, MAY 2015.

EMILY AND MITCHELL'S GRADUATION FROM BELMONT UNIVERSITY, NASHVILLE TN, MAY 2015.

MATTHEW'S GRADUATION FROM NORTH DAKOTA STATE COLLEGE OF SCIENCE, MAY 2017. PHOTO TAKEN WITH PRESIDENT DR. JOHN RICHMAN AND WIFE MARCIA, MATTHEW'S CONFIRMATION MENTORS AND CLOSE FAMILY FRIENDS.

MAX, LEADING THE CREW DOWN MAIN STREET /
THE FIRST RUN WITH RANDY, NOVEMBER 2014.

MAX AT HIS "DOGGY SPA," BATHTUB OF
DARLENE AND STEVE, OCTOBER 2

FAMILY AND CLOSE FRIENDS
HONORING RANDY'S 53RD
BIRTHDAY AT BUCK SAW
LODGE, AUGUST 2015.

RICHMAN AND
BERNDT FAMILIES
AT THE OPENING
OF THE SEASON
FOR BISON MEN'S
BASKETBALL,
NOVEMBER 2014.

JANA AND THE LESNAR GIRLS IN AFRICA FOR A MISSION TRIP, WHICH OFFICIALLY OPENED THE CHILDREN'S ACADEMY IN THE VILLAGE OF KIBEHO, RWANDA, MAY 2018.

EDELWEISS COOKING SCHOOL CLASS DURING A "BUCKET-LIST" SOUND OF MUSIC TOUR TO AUSTRIA. PICTURED: MOM, KATHY, TYLER, AND JANA, NOVEMBER 2016.

ONE OF MANY OUTINGS WITH THE BUCK SAW LODGE FAMILY, HEADED TO SEE CHRIS TOMLIN AND MATT MAHER IN CONCERT IN THE TWIN CITIES, OCTOBER 2017.

A FAMILY TRIP TO
WACO TEXAS, FALL 2018.

THE BUCK SAW
LODGE FAMILY
PHOTO TAKEN AT
NIECE KATE'S AND
CORY'S WEDDING IN
ALEXANDRIA MN,
SEPTEMBER 2018.

DEDICATION OF THE
RUN WITH RANDY
MEMORIAL GARDEN,
AUGUST 2017.

MITCHELL AND EMILY
(BERNDT) STEELE,
JANA, TYLER, AND
MATTHEW, FALL 2018.

EXTENDED BERNDT FAMILY PHOTO TAKEN DURING
THE CHRISTMAS CELEBRATION, DECEMBER 2018.

EXTENDED SIPE FAMILY PHOTO, TAKEN AT GRANDMA
SIPE'S BIRTHDAY CELEBRATION, SEPTEMBER 30, 2018.

Forty-eight

Summer for the Sipe family was always, and continues to be, a season when golf takes a front seat right next to the lake time, I suppose.

Since early in my banking career, I had organized the annual Bremer Charity Golf Tournament. While golf was not a sport Randy took up until later in his adult life, it was a pastime he thoroughly enjoyed, particularly when it involved my family. He had much to learn from them to improve his score. But he was a golf enthusiast, nonetheless: books, "Golf Magazine," the latest and greatest golf gear. Randy would put together a team that always included my dad as his partner.

The first year after his funeral, the tournament went by in a blur. But the second year gave me a bit of trouble.

Like other meaningful events to this point, I planned the details. What could I do to make the day more tolerable? I called my dad to ask him to participate—this time with me as his partner. I invited Kathy and her husband, Jim, to join us.

Not a true golfer, I could eke out a decent score. Always on the organizing end, this was the first time I experienced the tournament from the team's side—the best medicine for an event that had disturbed my sleep as I worried how I might get through the day. Our team recorded a competitive score, enough to get us in the money. And I racked up another event without Randy.

Golf healed my heart that sunny June day.

• • • • • • • •

As Independence Day approached, I remembered Randy's bright smile as he handed out ice cream cones from the front pontoon at the boat parade.

Always a summer highlight, this year the July holiday ran smack into my parents' sixtieth wedding anniversary. Our extended family gathered to reminisce with Mom and Dad about their love story, which had begun when they were kids in high school. We all agreed: they continue to be a living example of love and commitment.

We pored over family pictures, the pinnacle of our gatherings, depicting all that my parents accomplished: four children, their spouses, twelve grandchildren and their spouses, even a great-grandchild.

With some encouragement, their grandchildren entertained us all by sharing favorite memories about Grandpa and Grandma.

As I watched Mom and Dad throughout the festivities, part of me felt removed, as though I was viewing them from a distance. A spectator witnessing their deep love, their tender care for each other. To have that great love for sixty years, a tribute of how lucky I have been to be their daughter.

When the band played Anne Murray's "Could I Have This Dance?," emotion slammed into me, hard and fast, as the echo of past conversations overlaid it all: Randy and I declaring our own lasting love, vowing to remain true as we grow old together. *Love you until the end of time.*

Embracing, Mom and Dad swayed on the deck as the crowd looked on. The siblings took their spouses by the hand and joined them. And it hit me … I was alone again.

Sensing my stabbing pain, Tyler grabbed me by the arm and escorted me to the deck.

He gets it! I thought. Warmth spread through me, touched that this man-child of mine understood and empathized with my silent agony even in the midst of this joyous day.

Choose gladness, Jana. Look how lucky you are! Your children, your own love story of marriage, your family and extended family, your friends! Choose joy.

Love stories, I decided, come in all forms and last forever. Regardless of death.

Forty-nine

Randy's fifty-fourth birthday came in August but not without some anxious moments and reluctant planning. Because the XXI Summer Olympics were being held in Rio de Janeiro, I thought it would be nostalgic to honor Randy's love of the games.

Our house on Maple Street had boxes crammed with VHS tapes of prior Summer Olympics that Randy would watch in his spare time. He could recite the winners, the losers, and even the times of world-class athletes for their running events. It was so fitting we would remember his birthday with a little friendly competition followed by steaks on the grill.

I would host the Berndt rendition of the Buck Saw Lodge Summer Olympics. A 5K around the lake front. Paddleboard races in and around the 100-foot dock. Running long jump on the soft, sandy beach. And some semblance of a water dive off Randy's beloved boat.

The first ever BSL Summer Olympics!

The finale took the cake. Max participated in his single event: springing long jump. He ran full speed along the extra-long dock, plunging into the water to retrieve his trophy—a tennis ball with the inscription, "Winner, winner, chicken dinner."

Laughter filled the beach ... punctuated by scattered tears of sadness and hugs of condolence. Not for losing the events, but for missing Randy—their dad, uncle, brother-in-law—so very much. Randy would have been first to the line that day to take on the challenge but, more importantly, he would have been the biggest cheerleader, watching his family give it their all.

Fifty

Fall flung a new flurry of sadness at me and caught me off guard. I had just come off a wonderful summer at the lake with lots of pleasurable family and friend time.

August had been a steamy month and the annual cross-country home meet was its typical hot, windy self. I volunteered at my usual post as the "turtle" for the meet—driving a golf cart around the course, tailing the end of the pack, picking up any stragglers having trouble in the heat … or victims of early-season plague: being grossly out of shape.

As my friend Diane and I puttered around the course, my mind wandered back to ten years earlier when Tyler was in cross-country. Watching him sprinting down the course that sweltering day, I wanted to shout, "You can stop, honey! I know it's too hot. It's okay, you can quit."

Laughing at myself later that year, I had realized my son was passionate about a sport I had never been involved with and I had a lot to learn if I was going to be Super Sport Mom Spectator. I would need coaching, the right words, the appropriate cheers.

"Run faster!" *Oops, don't yell that.*

"You can do this!" *Not want he wants to hear.*

"Looking good, Tyler, looking good!" *Obviously a mom-stumble.*

Randy took me in hand, taught me what comments moms are allowed to make—none of which I'd come up with on my own. Finally, I shut my mouth and took out my camera. Photos, that's what I could do to support!

But now, when Coach Lasch asked if I would assist at the awards ceremony, I took on a new responsibility. As the season's top runners received their prizes in front of supportive coaches, family, friends, and community spectators, I handed out tee-shirts. A sense of pride quickened my pulse and made my smile genuine. As wife to the late Coach Berndt, I savored the honor.

Coach Lasch read his prepared speech about Randy's impact on the sport, the team, the community. He surprised me with an announcement. Going forward, the home meet would be titled the "Randy Berndt Memorial Cross Country Meet."

I was unprepared for Coach Lasch's kind words and over-the-top praise for my husband—stretching back years in time. Caught by surprise, I was speechless. Once again, Randy had shown up, filling my cup with enough joy to carry me through the next months.

All season, I kept an eye on their cross-country results and eventually hosted the team for a pre-sectionals dinner. My heart warmed as I listened to their chatter about the races … and even a few Coach Berndt memories. I fed their stomachs, but they fed my soul.

● ● ● ● ● ● ● ●

Matthew returned to North Dakota State College of Science

for his second year, setting his sights on a spring graduation from the junior college and stirring up feelings and emotions I should have been accustomed to by now. After all, autumn had a history of putting me into a funk—starting the year I left home. In 1980, I took off for Concordia College, leaving my comfortable northern Minnesota community of Crookston. When Mom dropped me off at the Park Region girls' dormitory in Moorhead, I thought my life would never be the same again. And it wasn't. Moving from a warm, beautiful, safe home to a cold, strange, scary dorm room.

I survived. I made it.

When I became a mom, my fall funk arose at the start of each school year. Bittersweet first-day pictures. Meeting teachers. Getting back into a routine. Change! Driving *my babies* to college. Wow, they certainly don't write about that experience in the what-to-expect-when-you're-expecting books I had read, cover to cover, and multiple times!

The first time we left Tyler at the dorm. Life-changing, for sure. Did I raise him right? Did he have all it takes to be successful? Then you come to the realization that it's all okay. It's all part of God's plan. He'll survive. He'll make it.

Another fall, my husband left his engineering career to teach. Change, again.

College for Emily. Now Matthew.

Time truly does march on. Nothing is stagnant. Nothing stays the same. Change is a given. And I wasn't exempt from the process.

It was fitting that Tyler urged us to sign up for another fitness challenge, taking us to new heights: the Twin Cities 10K. He suggested it could be my birthday gift from him. He would take care of registration and the associated fees.

All sounded good to me at the time we talked, but when the weekend arrived so did my pattern of regret and doubt. Why had I agreed to this?

Tyler underplayed the commitment, reminding me I walk

every day, many days for forty-five minutes or more.

"Mom, after you walk you hardly even breathe heavy. You're in the best shape of your life."

Tyler was a cheerleader, just like his dad. How could I disappoint him? Besides, it was a gift, my birthday present.

So we gathered that crisp fall morning—Tyler, Matthew, and his girlfriend, Ali, and I, sporting our Run with Randy tees—on the lawn of the Minnesota state capital to race in my first ever 10K. There was something exciting about being in the big city along with thousands of other runners and serious walkers, taking our first mile towards the Basilica, St. Paul's largest Catholic church. Sunshine glittered on the steeple, sending chills down my spine.

Well, aren't you lucky, Jana. You're here with family. You have your health.

"And I have my God," I whispered under my breath.

Contentment washed into my heart, seeping into all the cracks, filling the empty corners. A new feeling for me. Or at least one I had not felt in a really, really long time.

The scenic route took us through spectacular sights and the race went much better than I had envisioned. I crossed the finish line with my niece and namesake, Annie, waving me in, an extra special moment.

Fifty-one

Late fall presented the long-awaited opportunity to take an international vacation with Tyler, Kathy, and my mom, who was now eighty years old and demanding her bucket list trip to Salzburg, Austria. So there you have it; if mom wanted it, I couldn't deny her that wish.

In preparation, I applied for a passport and visited a travel nurse to ensure I had all the proper vaccinations. With the green light to travel and passports in hand, we departed on our seven-day adventure.

Throughout our childhoods, Kathy and I watched "The Sound of Music" annually during the Christmas holiday—until we eventually owned the VHS and later the DVD so we could watch it as many times as we wanted. Austria wasn't only our mother's dream destination. It had been in the making for decades and was coming to fruition at last.

We climbed the hills of Salzburg. We belted out the familiar songs memorized years ago. We took a "Sound of Music" tour of the city. The getaway, a dream-come-true for us all, was a needed break from the single life I was still trying to navigate. It gave me the chance to lose myself in new sights and scenes.

Traveling in a foreign country, where the language was completely unfamiliar, opened my mind to a new world. A world far removed from anything I had ever lived. I opened myself to new cultures, new food, new experiences.

Occasionally, I found myself so distracted and delighted ... that I forgot my burdens back home. Each time guilt tried to tiptoe in, I shut the door in its face. Firmly.

At Edelweiss Cooking School, I learned to whip up a fragrant apple strudel. I managed to board a train to the lavish Neuschwanstein Castle. I toured the sobering Dachau Concentration Camp Memorial near Munich.

I saw and visited and absorbed. I was a single woman traveling to places I'd only read about in books.

The trip was the start of new chapter for me.

Danke schön, Austria.

Fifty-two

More and more, I began thinking about how I wanted to remember Randy and, equally, how I might create a legacy in his honor.

Dr. Seuss wrote, "Sometimes you will never know the value of a moment until it becomes a memory."

How could I keep memorializing my husband? The options, I learned, were endless—and the community jumped right in ahead of me.

His cross-country team raised money to have a special tree planted on the corner of the school grounds. As a family, we judiciously selected his favorite sugar maple, knowing that every fall the tree would boast richly red and orange leaves. Its vibrant colors would draw attention, a sure reminder of Randy and what he meant to so many of his students, athletes, and fellow educators.

Various unique opportunities arose for us to buy and engrave Randy's name on a memorial brick or block to be placed in a new park or the walkway of a civic building. This was an appealing way to keep his name in permanent locations in the community.

The most touching memorial was a large boulder placed on the other corner of Breckenridge Elementary and Middle School, where my husband attended, graduated, and taught for many years. "Run with Randy Memorial Gardens" was etched into the marker.

Cards continued to arrive bearing money "to use as we saw fit" to keep Randy's memory alive. Initially, I was not prepared to put the time and energy into researching what this might be. But, as time passed, I wanted to do something for the high school where Randy had coached. Or possibly something involving his passion for running. Obviously, his impact on our community was astounding and deserved to live on in some way.

Several months after Randy's death, I approached Diane, the superintendent of schools.

"So many people have sent money," I explained, "requesting that it be used as a lasting legacy. Do you have ideas for me? Ways it might enhance or add to the school?"

After consideration, she suggested a project to improve the bell tower at the entrance of the school grounds.

As the project started to come together, I visited with several former students of the school district. Many shared fond memories and cute stories about the role of the bell during their school years. The site held a special significance and meaning to them. It was the "cool spot" to meet. Sometimes it marked the tender moment where flirting occurred, a new friendship formed, a first kiss found its mark. Sometimes it was the place to settle a score.

Run with Randy Memorial Gardens were designed around the bell tower, created and dedicated in loving memory of my husband. This space would come to hold a special feeling for all us. I found myself walking by the school and the bell tower often, my heart warming with memories of such a special man.

Fifty-three

My marriage to Randy was so much more than a lifelong commitment to be his wife and to love him unconditionally. While that was certainly part of it, marriage united us, made us "one" just as God intended. We connected in incomparable ways that no other relationship could ever exceed. That's the beautiful design of marriage.

Oh, we each still had our own identity, and aspects of our lives were ours alone, but marriage entwined us. You know how it is. My friends become *our* friends, his money becomes *our* money, my house becomes *our* house, his church becomes *our* church. After years of marriage, we all start acting, thinking, and speaking like each other. So close was our thinking, so deep our understanding of each other, it was not uncommon for me to finish sentences for Randy! It was as though we knew what the other was going to say before the words came out of our mouths.

We were tangled together, and one of the more abstruse yet

challenging steps I took in the second year was untangling myself.

What do you do when the one with whom your entire life is entangled is suddenly gone? It feels like half of you was ripped away. Now I was a single unit and needed to think and be and do for myself. I needed to figure how to separate my life from his or, maybe, from his memory.

It was like tugging a comb through tangles in your hair, or unsnarling the delicate chain to a favorite necklace, or unknotting a stubborn shoestring. The process sometimes was painful and tedious and frustrating.

Oftentimes, it was a big punch in the gut.

Learning to fall asleep alone in my queen-sized bed—when I was accustomed to the warmth of Randy's body next to mine, his breath reassuring in my ear.

Always being in the driver's seat, no matter the depth of Minnesota snow or the slickness of ice or my fatigue—when I had contentedly spent decades as co-pilot.

Washing and drying dishes solo—when it took half the time with my kitchen teammate.

Grilling meat— when I used to watch the pride he took in that job.

Without knowing how or the exact moment this tugging apart first started, I realized I had processed a thought through my own perspective—without considering what Randy would think or how "we" might have thought differently at one time. It was a profound "I" moment. My worldview had shifted under my feet and I felt it. A subtle shift, yes, but a shift toward being my own self.

What I had dedicated my life to for twenty-eight years was gone, and I was untangling into a culture that catered to couple-dom. With Randy's death, I plunged into the table-for-one phase. The "Jana & Guest" phase. I was the remaining half of "Randy and Jana Berndt." My new, shorter address labels shouted it out for all to see: JANA Berndt!

Woman alone. No more "and" for me.

I prayed I would always have a connection to Randy. I never want to forget how it felt to be his wife and the special way he looked at me, only me. I never want to forget how it felt to be the mother of his children. He was an amazing man and each of them carry a part of him in their looks, their mannerisms, their characteristics. I want to remember how his voice sounded. And his infectious laugh. I never want to lose the warmth of his hand in mine.

Another part of separating myself from Randy meant venturing into the world as a single person. I would attend weddings solo, funerals without a spouse, community hotspots dateless.

Prior to the first wedding, I asked the bride's mother about the guest list and learned of several other single women who would attend. I sought them out at the ceremony and casually joined them as we walked to the reception. I appeared confident and capable. But, unable to handle it, I excused myself before the couple's wedding dance and drove home early.

This was also the time when I was forced to explore the world outside my workplace and home. My job required me to attend bank events and community functions like the Chamber of Commerce banquet or the hospital fundraiser. Faced with the thought of a public appearance, I had to psych myself to participate. Not yet my typically outgoing self, feeling guarded in circles I was exploring, nonetheless I made an appearance. I was grateful to have a strong support system of co-workers who wouldn't even give me an option to attend alone.

The first college alumni association fundraising event was brutal, having previously attended each year with Randy at my side. I purchased the ticket, bought a new party dress, indulged in a pedicure and manicure—just as I'd done in the past. I was ready for a night on the town.

Marcia and John had made arrangements to escort me to the evening event; I was a guest at their table and felt comfortable engaging in small talk with colleagues, community leaders, friends, and acquaintances. Simple. Benign.

Until emotion overtook me and I lost my confidence.

Excusing myself, I pressed through the crowd and secluded myself in the restroom, where I hoped to regroup and pull myself together.

I can't pretend anymore. It's just too much to expect of me.

Being in public where everyone seemed strong and confident, their lives in order and their families whole and happy was a stark contrast that pressed on me. I wasn't strong; I wasn't confident. My life wasn't in order. And my family certainly was not whole and happy without Randy.

I texted Matthew, who was out with friends for the evening, and asked if he could come get me. I slipped out the side entrance, texted Marcia to explain my abrupt departure, and slid into the passenger seat. We drove home in silence. I had failed. I had quit. Would I ever be able to go out in public again?

When morning came, I revisited the prior evening, rolling my reaction through my mind.

You didn't really fail, I reassured myself. *And you're certainly not going to throw in the towel.*

But I accepted that it was going to be a slow process. I could not return to life in the fast lane quite as quickly as I had hoped. Too much had changed. Too much was left to overcome.

Even so, I congratulated myself. I had taken a step forward, even if it was a small one.

As I continued to "go public," I accepted the untangling that could only occur by me. I was the only person who could possibly separate the strands or pick apart the tight knots of my marriage to Randy. As painful as it was, I needed to become "unmarried."

I'd like to say that the pain of untangling ended when I learned to be in public alone and finally took off my wedding ring. The truth of the matter is that there were—and likely always will be—more hurdles to vault.

Fifty-four

After graduating from college in 1984, I had moved to Breckenridge, a cozy community of 3,500 where I knew no one even close to my age. I was scared and lonely. Thankfully, my first "real" job at a local bank kept me occupied and socialized during the day, but at night, when I returned to my empty apartment, I was alone. Oh, I made a few friends and tried my best to fit in around town but, at the end of the day, when it was time to crawl into bed, it was still just me.

After six months, I met Randy Berndt. I had found my person! I was no longer alone. It was the start of entangling my life with another's and I treasured the lusciousness of it all.

A short twenty-eight years later I reencountered that early sense of floundering alone in a sea of strangers. This second time around, I realized I still wasn't good at being on my own. I still didn't like cooking for one and despised eating by myself. I'd never conquered my uneasiness over those strange "sounds that go bump in the night." I despised evenings by myself, frightened of possible intruders. I dreaded the restless sleep that confronted me in bed. The fact was I didn't like how it feels to be untangled.

Already learning the importance of grace and baby steps, I started small and simple: A white-noise tower fan kept the scary "bump in the night" sounds at bay. I swapped my evening television schedule for a good book to help me relax and lay a foundation for a peaceful night's sleep. The installation of a home security system reassured me and instilled a sense of safety. After all, even the brashest intruder would be dissuaded by a loud alarm!

I didn't have to look far to find someone willing to share a meal with me. Matthew was an agreeable dinner companion most weekday nights. But for him, college was on the horizon. And there would come a day when others wouldn't be able to join me for dinner, and I'd have to eat alone, a situation that needed to be resolved.

I clicked on the television. "Wheel of Fortune" provided rousing mealtime company. As I grew more confident being alone, I made it through meals at the breakfast nook by myself. While I wouldn't say I mastered the process, I found myself getting less lonely each time I sat there. Creating a new routine in a new space afforded an opportunity to see and experience things from a different angle. Much better than existing exclusively in the world of the-way-it-used-to-be.

Each solution solved a problem. Each change marked a milestone on the Highway to Singledom. Each shift equaled a small sign of resilience and independence. Even though I wished with all my being that I didn't have to live this way, I felt a sense of pride in my accomplishments.

Most unexpected was the jolt I encountered at church.

Randy and I had spent all our dating and married years at United Methodist, where we were highly involved in various ministries, often alongside each other. Randy served on various leadership boards and taught Sunday School for many years. He mentored many kids and willingly shared his faith with others. I was the church pianist and co-led many musical groups both during the week and on weekends. Randy, too, was involved in the music program, singing in the choir, participating in the choir cantata and praise band. In addition, he was supportive of my music involvement, often becoming the "crew" when we took our music on the road.

Every Sunday, without fail, you would find the Berndt family sitting in the second pew on the side of the church nearest the piano. I would provide prelude music. The kids would trickle in after Sunday School and Randy would greet the members of the congregation while making his way to his seat. Even when the kids were younger, Randy would sit with them in our pew while I played the piano a few feet away.

Our kids were baptized, confirmed, and graduated from the church programs. We were enmeshed in our church community. Attending together was a high priority for our family.

After Randy's death, I continued to attend and participate, but his absence was even more obvious on Sunday morning. I fought tears at each service, moisture clouding my vision until reading music was nearly impossible. At times, the pain of his absence won; salty tears streamed down my cheeks and dripped onto the piano keys as I played. Difficult Sunday after difficult Sunday, I forced myself to push through, certain it would become easier with time.

It didn't.

After a year had passed, my distress was as debilitating as ever. Each time I looked at the Berndt pew, all I saw was emptiness. Tyler and Emily, of course, were at their homes in the Twin Cities and Nashville. Although Matthew still attended with me most weeks, my constant companion no longer did. His place on the pew was bare, a hollow empty space.

I especially dreaded the moment the congregation recited The Lord's Prayer. At this point in the service, Randy and I always joined hands. Literally tangled together like that, we created a peaceful, united moment as we prayed in unison—as one—words we both wholeheartedly believed. It was too painful to endure this week after week without Randy, every service a reminder of all we had lost.

So when Marcia invited me to attend her church during the Lenten season, I didn't hesitate. The change of scenery didn't make me miss Randy less, but the fresh environment wasn't as painful of a reminder. I didn't find myself looking for him and searching the pews for his face. I eventually reached out to the pastor, who came to visit me at the house. Kind and understanding, she, too, had endured a great loss in her life when her fiancé passed away before their wedding. We forged a nice connection as we shared a deep understanding of grief and how hard it is to move beyond mourning.

As we talked and prayed, I acknowledged my need for a new beginning. I needed a fresh start. I needed a new church home that would be mine alone. The difficult decision to leave United Methodist was complicated further because of my dear friends there and irreplaceable memories entwined throughout the decades. That church cupped our family's history in the palms of its hands. Mercifully, while our pastor assured me I would always be welcome, he understood that I needed to take this excruciating step to untangle and move forward.

Fifty-five

I looked at my hand, tilting it until the light caught the row of diamonds on the band. It glittered as brightly as it had in the case at Wimmer's Diamonds. I loved my ring. Baguettes lined the sides of the large princess-cut diamond, a stunning upgrade from my original set. And even more precious than any of the rings I posted on my Pinterest board, which had been growing for several years.

The store manager was thorough, kind, and helpful as we meticulously selected just the right one. She answered each of Randy's detailed questions about quality, clarity, and size. I learned more about diamonds that day than I ever expected. Such a memorable shopping trip together, especially since my first ring had been a surprise.

We picked it out for our twenty-fifth wedding anniversary—platinum, a nod to the time-honored silver anniversary. I loved what the ring symbolized: marriage. And I loved being married. It showed the world I was Randy's wife, and I loved being his wife.

I was the bride who never, ever, planned to take off her ring. I slept in it, showered in it, gardened in it—a permanent fixture on my fourth finger. So I had no predetermined plan, no specific time or deadline for removing it. In fact, early on I could see myself wearing the ring forever. What harm would it do? I loved it and all it represented.

So, why now?

The answer was simple. The answer was complicated.

Simply, it was part of my process to detangle. On a deeper level, I felt pressured to remove it. I had been asked several times about my ring—even by a complete stranger.

"You're still wearing your wedding ring. How long have you been a widow?"

How dare someone even ask? I fumed. *It's no one's business but mine.*

During a deep conversation about my foggy future, a friend asked if I was ready to consider dating.

"Yes." My comment was confident, unhesitant.

Her eyebrow lifted. "Are you sure?"

"Oh, yes. I'd like to find a friend to do things with."

She pointed at my hand. "Jana, you're still wearing your wedding ring. I'm not so certain anyone will be ready to ask you out when they see that ring on your finger."

Her words haunted me and kept me awake a few nights until, reluctantly, I decided it was time to release myself from the safety of the ring.

Or, at least try. I could always slip it back where it belonged.

Both hands trembled as I slid the ring off my finger. My hand felt naked, bare and foreign. I felt its absence as surely as I felt Randy's, a sense of loss and missing. The startlingly white indentation left behind was a metaphor for the lasting impression our marriage had left on my heart. We had pledged for permanency, until "death do us part."

But Death had fulfilled his calling and parted us.

The initial trial lasted several months and eventually felt like it was meant to be. The bare white band of skin encircling my finger showed signs of a tan, and the indentation began to fill in over the next several months—never quite disappearing. A subtle sign that something used to be there, a tender part of who I am.

I knew that, when the time was right and nudging me, I'd find a perfect, permanent spot for "our" ring.

(A few years later, I would run across the ring I loved so much. Curiously, I would slip it on my finger, surprised at the unnatural weight of it, the foreignness, and try to imagine myself wearing it again. In that moment I would know I was fully untangled and I would feel oddly free.)

Fifty-six

Everybody likes a party, unless it's a pity party. As I
went about separating myself from life-with-Randy and grieving
a significant loss, I started a fresh litany of "Why me, God?"
questions. The trap was open wide and easy to fall into.

On my drives home from work, I sometimes indulged in
three-minute pity parties. If my sister answered her phone when
I called, I invited her to the party, too, as I vented, cried, and felt
sorry for myself in general. Kathy showed grace and understanding.
I needed both.

Filled with quality family and couple time, Friday nights
had been my favorite time of the week before Randy died. Now,
they heralded a dreary weekend ahead. After all, what did I have to
look forward to?

The ongoing temptation to pity myself was real and felt
justifiable in so many ways. Reality, harsh and frank, spotlighted my
companionless existence.

What I needed to come to grips with were the self-defeating thought patterns that did not promote joy. And, despite my current circumstance, I was deeply committed to keeping joy around. So I would promise myself that by the time I parked the car in the garage, the party was over. Done. Kaput. Even if that required another spin around the block to finish my weeping. When I swiped away the tears and climbed out of the car, it was time to find and focus on the good. The positive.

Choose joy, Jana. Choose joy!

Just because I was choosing joy, however, didn't mean that I liked the reality of going home to an empty house for the weekend. Even though I accepted it as my new norm, I didn't like it, not one bit. Nothing about it promoted feelings of joy. Or, as I described it to a friend one Friday afternoon, "I have no one to do nothing with."

The phrase "working for the weekend" held new meaning. I saw it as a *workout* to the loneliness of the weekend. A test of my commitment to avoid a lifelong pity party of one.

I knew that a friend or relative was only a phone call away, but that required an extra step that, sometimes, I didn't want to take. Social engagements of that sort involved connecting, planning, coordinating schedules … effort. Even though I knew it was healthy to reach out, there were times when I didn't want to expend the energy required. Not when "doing nothing" with Randy used to be so easy and effortless. So many times I was too tired or too fragile to find something to do, something to fill my weekend. And there was only so much housework, so many special projects and activities around the house to keep me busy. When they were done, what then?

I missed those nights when we had nothing planned but to just … be. To watch a movie. Read. Putter. Do nothing.

Yet, I wasn't alone. Matthew didn't require any effort on my part to converse or entertain. It was simpler for my son and I to sit in silent companionship.

"No one to do nothing with," was a sad reality of my life after the loss of my husband.

I encountered the drowning weight of loneliness even in a room full of people. I tried to lighten the burden by reminding myself how lucky I was to have had a complete family, a loving husband for nearly three decades. I tried to trust the journey God was guiding me through. It was tough to retrain my mind. It's called "training" for a reason; it isn't easy and it takes time to get good at it!

Eventually, I found the solution: gratitude.

When self-pity threatened to spiral out of control, I started asking myself to find one or two things to be thankful for today— just today—and jotted them in my journal. Over time my jottings expanded into a list, eventually nudging me to accept the obvious: I really had so much to be grateful for. Even on the mornings when I awoke to a whirlwind of emotion, I sought out something, anything to appreciate. "I'm grateful for the sun shining into my bedroom window to wake me before my alarm clock." Or "I'm grateful for Max's thumping tail outside my bedroom door."

A quick moment of thankfulness started my days. Gratitude pulled me back from the perilous pit. My attitude, always a choice, lifted and a newly directed positivity lightened my load.

While Randy was in the hospital, our family started a journal to record all the blessings of the week. We knew the outcome for Randy was going to come with a temporary goodbye and a going home for him. But even as we witnessed the painful end to his earthly life, we witnessed many beautiful blessings during our final moments together. Journaling kept us centered on the good things in our life and produced a sense of thankfulness for all that we had. It kept us from focusing too narrowly on our losses and from worrying about those things beyond our control.

Creating my own journal came naturally. Although I still fought negative thoughts and feelings, reincarnating a practice of gratitude detoured me from overindulging in self-pity.

Meanwhile, I skirmished with that evil enemy ...
Comparison. When I held myself up against others, my life next
to theirs, I saw flaws and holes in mine and smooth perfection in
others. Obviously, I had been handed the short end of the stick.

Comparison surrounded me: couples holding hands, a
husband slipping his arm around his wife at the movie or gallantly
opening her car door or hugging and kissing her goodbye.

Even the opposite was painful: criticisms whispered in my
ear about spouses who, in some fashion or another, didn't meet
a minor expectation. Truly? Who shares those comments with a
freshly-minted widow? I would have given anything to have my
husband still here, to actually have these petty annoyances rather
than the permanent issues I faced daily.

"Really?" I wanted to say. "At least your husband is alive
for you to complain about."

Instead, I always bit my tongue.

As difficult as it sometimes was, I worked at taking those
negative threads and spinning them into gratitude, determined to
find joy in the midst of loss. Remembering our own wedding and
the wonderful years we had as newlyweds. Thinking about the times
Randy walked back into the house to make sure he had hugged and
kissed me goodbye and the times I pulled into the garage to find him
waiting to haul bags of groceries up the stairs ... the little moments
that made my heart swell.

Encouraging my thoughts to drift to these memories pulled
me out of a comparison mode and into gratitude.

This process and shift in thinking was not easy; oftentimes
it was downright unnatural. It didn't happen overnight and I had
plenty of moments where I was in the pity-party mood. I lost
more than one battle with Comparison. But I can't say it enough:
Gratitude was the secret weapon.

But I knew comparison and self-pity were neither healthy
nor productive. Gratitude was the secret sauce and, while it certainly
didn't take the sadness away, the less I looked at others' lives and

the more I searched for good in my own—my thinking was altered.

No matter how tough my trials, there was always something to be grateful for. I just had to stretch myself and look for it.

Fifty-seven

"God will not give you more than you can handle."

Like you, I've heard this reassuring thought many times through the years. But it counters the lessons I absorbed in Sunday School. The Bible is full of stories about God calling ordinary people to do extraordinary deeds—deeds far beyond anything they could handle on their own. Look at Jonah, swallowed by a fish and lived to tell the tale. And what about Noah, building an ark and loading all those animals? How did he get them to cooperate? (He certainly didn't have a contrary dog named Max!) And the ultimate story of an ordinary woman named Mary who gave birth as a virgin.

God will not give you more than you can handle.

I had grabbed hold of this popular belief and clasped it like a lifeline throughout any hardships I encountered in my life.

In 2002 my dad survived two heart attacks and a quintuple bypass heart surgery. I paced the halls of Abbott

Northwestern Hospital repeating, "God won't give you more than you can handle." Half prayer, half incantation, the words played an endless loop in my mind as I tried to convince myself that all would be fine.

More than once that week of my dad's hospitalization, I pleaded with God to take this trial from me; it was more than I can handle.

You have me on a ledge God. I can't do this.

God showed up and brought healing for my dad and my family. As it turned out, He hadn't given us more than we could handle!

Yet, as time moved on and I experienced other challenges in my life, I began to question the validity of that saying. Was it really about what I can or cannot handle?

God doesn't spend His time setting up roadblocks, challenges, hardships—or the death of a spouse. Life tosses those things haphazardly at us. We live in a world where all kinds of things happen—some as the result of the choices of other people outside our control. Struggles of every shape and size lie around the corner, waiting to spring out and shout, "Boo!"

Life … happens. No one gets out of here without some bumps and bruises along the way. God doesn't hand us a plate of suffering or hard times. God is a good Father, who gives only good gifts to His children. Most importantly, he gives us the courage, strength, and faith to handle whatever life hands us, as long as we believe, rely, and trust in Him.

With man this is impossible, but with God all things are possible. (Matthew 19:26, NIV)

Randy's death realigned my perspective and opened my eyes to the misguided theory I'd clung to in the past. God did not cause Randy to have a heart attack. It just happened. God, all seeing and all knowing, knew this would happen and, thankfully, also knew what I would need to make it through this tragedy. Not only did He give me enough to make it through, He worked things out for our good. God gave me courage, strength, and the faith that *He* would carry me through this difficult time.

And at the end of anything and everything, isn't that really all we will ever need? A good God carrying us through life?

As my friend, Pastor Jen, counseled, "Jana, God does not guarantee that by following Him we won't have hardships. But what He does promise us is that as we follow Him, He will give us the fortitude to face life's hard times. This is what we call grace. A gift we don't have to earn."

When I mulled over this truth, it took root and resonated deep in my heart. Through all I had endured, God was with me. Accepting His help and constant presence better prepared me for the hardship I had *yet* to endure. I was able to clearly see that *His love carried me.*

One evening, I pored over an online article by pastor, author, and filmmaker Erwin McManus. A particular sentence stuck with me: "We have to stop pretending that faith makes life easier. Your faith doesn't make life easier, it makes you stronger."

Strength comes from faith, I mused. *Is my faith strong enough to sustain me? Can it get me through whatever is ahead?*

I contemplated the past and all that had happened.

Around and near the time of Randy's death, my dad experienced tightness in his chest, shortness of breath, and strong signs of additional heart problems. He shrugged them off, knowing he had to be strong for me and for my family. I only learned later that his pain and concerns were severe, the threat of another heart attack lurking in his mind. He postponed a doctor visit just long enough to get back to his regular cardiologist, who discovered additional blockage. After an angiogram and stents, all was resolved. God's hand had been around his heart.

Several weeks after the funeral, Tyler was heading home from a gym in downtown Minneapolis. When he proceeded through an intersection, a vehicle ran a red light and t-boned his brand new Honda Pilot. By God's grace and protection, Tyler was not injured and walked away from his totaled car. Without a scratch or bruise.

Only months after moving into the Crescent Street house, I returned after an evening out and noticed a light left on in the basement.

That's odd, I thought. *I don't recall the last time I was down there. Matthew must have been down and forgot to flip the switch.*

I opened the basement door and spotted water at the base of the steps. Odd, what would that be from? As I slowly walked down for a closer look, I heard a strange sound, like water running or spraying.

"Matthew," I yelled, "we have a water problem. Help!"

I turned the corner and saw the hot water heater spewing from all sorts of angles. And I had no idea where the water valve was.

This is Randy's responsibility, not mine!

Panicking, I raced upstairs to grab my cell phone and call Kent. Without knowing the layout of our basement, he calmly walked me through where the valve might be and what it would look like. As we followed his instructions, Matthew located the turnoff valve and finally stopped the flow. Our water heater was kaput.

Despite the late hour, Kent called Schmitty's Plumbing and Tim, the owner, came to check it out for me. All was safe and sound by 11:30, and he assured me he'd have a new one installed the next morning.

In bed, the experience replayed through my mind. Why was the basement light on? How had I noticed it peeking under the door? As I prayerfully thanked God for Kent's competent response to my phone call and the plumber's thoughtful visit to calm a worried widow, I saw that God had been there in the details. Helping me grow in my faith. Teaching me to trust Him more than I had ever known possible.

Fifty-eight

The second year crawled toward the finish line, but not without a celebration.

Adding to our ribbons and medals, the kids and I sprang at the chance to take our Run with Randy on the road. We gathered with family, friends and others to "Finish the Run" at Boom Island Park, the home of the annual event where our community remembered another great runner, David Forster.

The three-hour drive to the race gave me windshield time to think about David, an avid marathon elitist, as well as my son Tyler's close friend and college roommate at St. John's.

Earlier that year, David had coached, raced with, and practically carried Tyler the final miles of the Portland Marathon. It was Tyler's first full marathon; understandably, he felt ill-prepared, especially given the rugged terrain of the Portland route. He and his wide circle of college friends had made the trek to continue their running escapades.

Just like David had warned, Tyler hit a wall as he closed in on the last few miles.

"Keep going without me, David," Tyler panted. "I'll see you at the finish line."

David refused. He stuck with Tyler, encouraging him all the way in. Their bond of friendship tightened. Like my son, I was nourished by David's example of loyalty.

That's what friends do, I thought, *help us when we're down and can't go on.*

Mine had done the same since Randy's death. We were both blessed.

As we drove closer to Boom Island Park, my thoughts jumped to June when I was with my sister and parents at Buck Saw Lodge, enjoying another spectacular Lake Ida sunset. Glistening shades of yellow, orange, and pink shimmered across the waters and painted a perfect picture—one of reasons I love evenings at our cabin.

I glanced toward the western sky and witnessed a breathtaking scene: As the sun drifted lower on the horizon, shadows created a distinct reflection of a cross stretching across the water.

"Look!" My voice hushed with awe as I pointed and grabbed my cell phone to capture the rare sight. "Look!"

Together we watched the miraculous cross fade into the lake.

Just as the reflection dissipated, my cell phone rang, and I could tell by the number on the screen it was Tyler. *Odd,* I noted, *he never calls on a Friday night.* Wasn't he at a St. John's reunion? My heart pumped a little faster as my mom's intuition worked overtime. I consciously slowed my breathing.

"Hello, Ty. What's up?"

No greeting from my son. Only silence.

"Tyler, is that you?" My heart rate jumped again. "Are you okay?"

"I'm okay, Mom, But it's David. He, he ...."

I didn't understand. "David? What about him?"

"I think, I think he's .... Mom? I think he's dead."

Another silence stretched the distance between us.

"Are you alone, Tyler? Is someone with you?" I could hear frantic in my voice, which had suddenly raised in volume, as though I needed to speak loudly to be heard. "Tyler? Tyler?"

What seemed like minutes later, he managed to tell me his friend Katie was there.

As the story unfolded, I learned that David had gone for a run near Boom Island Park prior to picking up Tyler for the team reunion at St. John's. Only he never arrived. Didn't even respond to Tyler's text messages and phone calls.

David had collapsed. Later that night, officials at Hennepin County Hospital pronounced him dead.

Another runner, gone. A perfectly healthy, marathon runner. No warning. No signs. Gone.

This was a low blow to Tyler after just coming off a year of dealing with his dad's fatal heart attack. I worried about my son's huge loss.

Later that weekend, I picked up my phone and opened the picture of Friday's sunset. The recorded time? Exactly 9:59 p.m., mere moments after David died. I marveled, recognizing it as more evidence of a God-is-in-the-details: a sunset cross, a sign He was there to carry us through another tragedy.

Now a few months later we had arrived at the site to memorialize David and his family. To "Finish the Run" for our loved ones.

Our family members wore their Run with Randy shirts and carried thoughts and memories of Randy the entire 5K. Tyler, well, Tyler ran a little extra hard that day for his dad and for David. It was a reminder to him and all of us that life is fragile. No guarantees. No promises.

At the dinner afterward with my kids and Kathy's family,

I pronounced the occasion a success. Not merely as an event to honor the two deceased runners, but as an indicator that we were survivors. Nostalgic and reflective, I patted myself on the back.

Congratulations! Look how far you've come. My gaze panned the room as a tiny smile lifted my lips. *Look how much stronger you are.*

I had discovered resilience.

Year Three

DISCOVERING RESILIENCE

· ·

Fifty-nine

Resilience: A word you may never hunt for in the dictionary ... unless you find yourself a widow. I was ... so I did.

My trusty Merriam-Webster defines resilience as "an ability to recover from or adjust easily to misfortune or change." This is an explicit definition of my life three years into widowhood.

As I found myself transitioning into a new stage, I began to really understand the essence of the word. *Resilience.* A deepening sense of satisfaction lifted my chin as I acknowledged and celebrated my singular accomplishments.

With each achievement, I had praised myself with *Wow, Jana, you did it!*

An inward strength, absent for some time, seeped back. I hardly remembered what it felt like to make a sound decision without second guessing myself. Or of being frozen in my ability even to make life's simplest choices.

Then I received a phone call with bad news so unthinkable

I wasn't sure I could absorb it or handle it without my mate by my side to share my distress.

My dear friend Diane—young, vibrant, healthy Diane—was diagnosed with cancer. The news shocked her and all who knew and loved her. Uneasy about a recurring pain in her abdomen, she made an appointment with her doctor. Suspicious test results led to an immediate surgery to determine the exact cause.

Cancer. Such a despicable diagnosis. But Diane was a champ as she endured surgery, chemo treatments, and the tedious follow-up care necessary for this type of cancer. Months after her last treatment she was given the all-clear sign. Diane was cancer-free, praise the Lord!

She obligingly kept her regular appointments in Fargo with the oncologist, always praying for—yet expecting—good news. This particular morning, Diane and I prayed together, through our typical text messages, for her routine checkup to go well. Periodically throughout the day, I checked my phone as I waited for her confirmation text that all was good. She finally called in the late afternoon with results directly contrary to our earlier prayers.

The cancer had returned.

I stared at the cellphone in my hand. *Does this mean what I think it does? Her cancer is not curable?*

Shock, dismay, and fear paralyzed me. Diane had become such an integral part of my inner circle; truthfully, she was the nucleus. I relied heavily on her as my sounding board, my personal encouragement coach.

Until this point, I had little experience with serious cancer. My grandma grappled with a short, three-week stint of cancer before passing away, but she was eighty-six and had lived a full life. A few parents of friends, some acquaintances, a smattering of co-workers had struggled with the Big C, but no one this close to me had suffered and fought through treatments like Diane had. This latest news devastated Diane and her family—and me, as I trekked alongside her.

At this low point of sadness and disbelief, I perceived a change within myself. I had grown and developed a surprising strength as a result of the past months. I was a different version of myself—Jana 2.0—more emotionally muscular and stalwart. Self-assurance pumped through me. I could deal with this. I could be there for Diane to support her however she most needed me.

I had become *resilient*.

A recent devotion I had read reinforced this awakening. It is in our state of suffering—me losing the love of my life, Diane coping again with cancer—that God does some of His greatest work. I didn't agree with her cancer. Diane didn't agree with it. And we certainly didn't like it one bit.

But He was growing our resilience.

This message encouraged me and led me to newfound strength. For me, resilience was the end game of my suffering.

Sixty

Minnesotans resign themselves to endure the brutal weather February inflicts each winter. For me, February gnaws at my middle until I ache with a pain that doesn't subside until after the fourteenth. Valentine's Day–the most ritualized, sentimental day to celebrate the one you love.

Once upon a time, Randy had been a Valentine Romeo, gracing me with red roses. Until one year we decided not to waste money on blossoms that last only a few days. After all, I didn't need flowers to know that Randy loved me dearly, right? When a beautiful bouquet arrived at my office the day *after* Valentine's Day, I arched a disbelieving brow and opened the card. The inscription said: *Just because I love you.* I laughed out loud. Flowers were definitely Randy's "love language," his way of showing me how deeply he cared.

In addition, our tradition included a special dinner where we exchanged gifts and cards (he always gave me *three*), a treasured celebration between me and my valentine.

Understandably, the first year was the most ruthless, but honestly the succeeding years weren't much easier. Days leading up to, during, and after all pointed to the great love I lost. Even after three years of enduring the flower-scamming, card-hogging, hyped-up day without my Randy, the pain of his absence was acute. The lovely holiday is now my least favorite of the year. On the upside, my adverse reaction has heightened my awareness of others who might be missing a beloved spouse.

What did warm my heart was Marcia's and John's continued kindnesses, making sure I wasn't alone on Valentine's Day. My kids, too, made extra efforts to ensure their mom had flowers on her desk at work. After all, isn't much of the flower scene a visual for others to see just how much you are loved?

Kathy and the Lesnar clan expanded their family tradition to include ours in their Valentine's Day weekend. Jim puts his top-chef skills to the ultimate test with lobster and steak. The meal, along with homemade valentines and special love treats to all present, lifts a permanently stained heart.

Staying away from Facebook and other social media channels during February shielded my emotions from being sucked into the ugly comparison game. Instead, I say extra prayers of gratitude for the great love that Randy and I once shared, a valuable reminder of my good fortune.

Sixty-one

As the months rolled by, widowhood startled me with a yearning I hadn't expected. I felt a gaping void, the pangs of longing for physical touch. I missed Randy's neck massages as he zipped my dress before an evening out. A short but meaningful exchange between lovers. I missed Randy's signature hugs, hugs that enveloped me and erased my doubts and made everything better. The hugs that left me feeling full, expanded, complete. I missed Randy holding my hand as we strolled with Max or sat together in church. A gesture so insignificant and natural and commonplace that I was shocked at the importance it now held. The loss it signified.

These sensory components, so natural and mundane and certainly taken for granted, rose in stature. I wasn't prepared for this kind of deprivation.

Certainly, there were those who shook my hand, patted me on the back, lightly hugged me hello and goodbye. Types of touch so impersonal that we give out casually, like pamphlets to an event, even to strangers. I pined for something deeper, more romantic. The conscious and unconscious touches shared by lovers.

In his book, *The 5 Love Languages,* Gary Chapman describes it best for me: not a bedroom touch or intimate touch, rather a touch that fosters a sense of security and belonging in a relationship.

As I reread his book from my new station, I realized that physical touch was a missing piece to my puzzled soul. But here's the hard part ... my strongest love language never was physical touch. Indeed, I spent so much of my life not subscribing to the need for physical touch, I was stunned at my sudden, desperate desire for it. Obviously, Randy had provided exactly what I had needed to feel fulfilled, although I had been unaware that I needed it. It rounded the edges of our marriage enough that now life felt dull and jagged. Splintered.

Outside of my inner circle of friends, family and children, personal touch comes sparingly. So a widow is left to wonder, to ponder her quandary. How does she fill that need? It's a tricky question and I'm still searching for answers. Let's just say the new Jana never turns down a long, heartfelt hug these days.

Sixty-two

It's human nature to mark time by events. Before college, after graduation. Before the engagement, after the wedding. Before the house sold, after the move. Using a death to mark time is no different.

Each time I recalled a memory or related a story, I found myself starting with, "Before Randy's death" or "Before November 1" or "After Randy died" or "After I was widowed." Somehow, that moment in time had become my ground zero, the point on the timeline of my life from which I either digressed backward or moved forward.

Isn't that how it is with all life-changing events? They impact us with a force so powerful that memory itself is born at those exact points. Their importance grows and swells until they consume all other happenings and, like insistent toddlers, shout, "Me first! Me first!" And we oblige and place them at the front of the line.

When I sorted through my mind to date a photo, remember an activity, or frame a thought, I placed myself at Randy's death. From there I decided which timeframe: before or after.

I look forward to the day that I can replace this pivotal place-marker with a happier circumstance. Maybe the day I'm a grandma? Or the day I retire to see the world? But, for now, I continue to use my husband's death to reference my life.

Sixty-three

By now I had gained a new appreciation for slowing down and simplifying. Thick in the midst of the rat race, Randy and I had juggled two fulltime, stressful jobs while raising three kids and actively participating in various community and church projects. Simple was not a word we used to describe our daily schedules.

Now, the picture looked quite different, yet it took all that change for me to realize that uncomplicated is good. Simple feels fine. Chaos does not necessarily equal happiness. My mental health and spiritual well-being required me to push on the brakes so I could figure out what *needed* to be done versus what I *wanted* to get accomplished because, clearly, my brain and energy were not in sync.

Mundane tasks, which just months ago felt like a strenuous mountain climb, eased and softened. Although manageable, each still required a distinct pause for me to evaluate and deliberate.

Put it in perspective, Jana, I reminded myself.

Was it a big deal? Was it eminent? Could it be postponed? Could it be ignored? What would happen if it never got done? Could someone else do it?

Considering these options infused me with a sense of control that I desperately needed. Even when it came to the bookwork.

In the Berndt household, I had always been the one who managed finances and most of the paperwork required to keep things running smoothly. Randy certainly had a slight interest in the checkbook balance but not so much in the details. These defined roles might have resulted from our upbringings or because of my profession in banking.

I ran our household from one checkbook, sharing the blanks as needed.

After a tiny squabble about money, Randy said, "It's my turn to take over the bills and balancing the checkbook."

"Fine by me," I said. Maybe then he would appreciate how tough it was to keep everything afloat.

After about two months of his tenacious efforts to tally the books, Randy reproached me.

"Do you know how much you spend on your hair and hair products?"

That was it; that was all it took as far as I was concerned. It was over. We were not going to survive marriage if he questioned and itemized to the degree of whether my hair supplies impacted the family budget.

Nothing more said, nothing more done.

We had very few arguments about money and how we spent it, but that short two-month experiment taught us both an important lesson about our roles in the family: You do what you do best and I'll do what I'll do best.

The art of paying bills and keeping it all in balance changed after Randy died. I suppose in large part because I began to simplify my lifestyle and our obligations. The preplanning we had done years earlier afforded me the opportunity to eliminate some of our debt and to pad my financial future, which altered the landscape of the monthly recordkeeping.

For the most part, I settled into a comfortable routine of typical paperwork needed to run a household.

The biggest nuisance was the paperwork resulting from furnace maintenance, yard care and upkeep, car repairs and services. This arena had been Randy's specialty, certainly nothing of interest to me. Fortunately, Matthew's college circumstance afforded him the opportunity to live at home on Crescent Drive. Because he commuted to campus for his four-year degree in finance, I was the grateful beneficiary. He was my almost full-time roommate.

With some trials and new boundaries set, the two of us got along well. Almost without notice, he shouldered the role of man-of-the-house—along with those irksome tasks I found so distasteful—while I continued on with my list of to-dos. Other than a few reminders that he is *not* my husband and that I am still his mom, the arrangement was a real blessing to me and my progression of untangling my life from Randy.

Except for those annoying telemarketers asking to speak to Randy Berndt. No matter how many times I politely asked them to remove his name from their lists, the phone calls continued. Disgusted, I finally pulled the plug and cut the cord to my landline. Once I canceled the service, the calls stopped. I no longer had to explain and remind myself of him not being here to take his own political survey calls.

Fewer calls, less stress.

Part of the transition to simplicity necessitated a change in thinking from "We can do that ourselves" to "We need help from others who know what they're doing."

I began to build a network of people I could trust, people I could go to for advice. Matthew topped my list along with my dad and John. They often pointed me to *their* experts.

A relationship with the Chevy dealership and general

manager, Joel, grew in importance. I simply could not risk car trouble when I traveled to the middle of North Dakota for work. My plumber, Steve, willingly gave me his cellphone number for household emergencies. I kept Willard, the furnace guru, on speed dial. Brian and Scott, co-workers and neighbors, had my back when it came to minor household concerns or extra-large snow piles.

The yard was a joint effort for Matthew and me. During the peak season, we spent several hours twice a week pushing the mower and riding the garden tractor. It was good exercise and wonderful outdoor time as we manicured the yard to his critical perfection. On the weeks Matthew wasn't around, I did my best to follow the faint lines still evident in the long blades of grass, gleeful that there were still a few things we could do ourselves.

Matthew coached me on the fine art of weed-whacking along the edges of the sidewalks, how to clean and park the mower in the garage, and the proper way to dispose of clippings. Part and parcel, I understood, of appreciating and understanding this fresh role reversal. Admittedly, I like driving the tractor yet I foresee a time when Matthew strikes out on his own and I need to use my ever-widening network to hire the job done. It may not be to Matthew's level of perfection, but acceptable to Jana's.

My expanding speed dial numbers will come in real handy as I forge ahead with this simplified lifestyle.

It has been reassuring and comforting to surround myself with a circle of people who make tasks more manageable. This evolved naturally, a skill I honed throughout my entire career. Building relationships has paid off in this single life I lead.

In the balance of maintaining independence while utilizing the skills of others, I miss being dependent on the man of my house, the man of my life. As much as I have grown to trust my network and inner circle, no one compares to the spouse who quietly assumed responsibility and effortlessly managed onerous duties. The burden of being the man *and* the woman of the house takes a toll on my mind and energy. Not to mention the time commitment it takes to keep your job performance topnotch, your house orderly inside and out, and your family humming like a well-oiled tractor. Simple. That's the final answer. Keep it simple.

Sixty-four

I'm grateful to say that I've made it through to the other side of some of my biggest initial challenges. I really feel that in a lot of ways, I've settled into my new life as a single woman.

Yes, I'm single. Again. I've come to accept this reality.

Even so, it stirs anxiety and worry of another sort. Will I stay single? Will I always be alone? Do I want another relationship? Will it be a waiting game or dating game?

And impending retirement adds to my confusion. What will I do after I leave the bank? Will I miss the structure of a job? How will I fill the open hours? Can I remain active in the community? Will retirement be meaningful without Randy? Is it possible to find a companion to share my passion for traveling?

The questions, large and loose and unanswered, wait around each corner to pounce on me. They float through my dreams like cartoon thought bubbles. I'm a single player squirming uncomfortably in a waiting game. Always a woman of action, I find this to be a season of spring waiting to burst forth and blossom. Is God testing my commitment to the virtue of patience?

He has blessed me with enough peace to understand that all things are temporary, even this time of indecision and uncertainty. It, too, will pass.

After making so many strides forward, I find myself open to meeting someone and admitting them into my life. A giant leap, I know. But the decision rests comfortably in my heart. Randy would want me to share my future with someone. A profound memory plays like a movie trailer through my mind.

One late cool fall evening a few days after his dad passed away, Randy and I were walking around the block. I felt particularly sad for his step-mom, Shirley, as she faced widowhood.

"I don't know what I would do if anything happened to you," I confessed, imagining myself in her situation.

With no hint of doubt in his voice, Randy responded, "I would want you to find someone else. I wouldn't want you to be alone."

Neither of us could have imagined the significance that conversation would have, but I hold on to those words as a sign that God is in control. He knew the moment would come when I would need to revisit those words from Randy's lips.

Randy gave me permission to move forward without him. His blessing to find a new norm.

· · · · · · ·

As a freshly minted college graduate a short thirty years earlier, I was working at my first adult job when a new opportunity presented itself in a different city: Breckenridge Minnesota. (Where on earth was that?) I couldn't wrap my mind around the concept of moving to someplace that felt so foreign. Despite my not-so-adventurous attitude—but perhaps to humor my parents, I applied, interviewed, and accepted the job within a few days. Things were moving much too swiftly considering I hadn't been serious about the possibility of a move. Now what?

I approached my dad, my go-to counselor for worldly decisions like this one. Certainly he would understand that I couldn't and shouldn't move away—especially to a strange community where I had no roots. We met at his office in the bank where, much to my dismay, we had an emotionally draining conversation that left me struggling with indecision. How could I leave all that was familiar and comfortable to go to a community where I knew absolutely no one?

Trembling with worry and uncertainty, I tried to look at the advantages: Unlike the job I currently held in Moorhead, this move offered me a chance at a banking *career*. My small town upbringing in Crookston and equally small college experience at Concordia equated to a sheltered life. This move would stretch me, every part of me.

With some parental encouragement and guidance, I decided to make the leap.

An early November move found me apartment hunting in Breckenridge—and renting in a somewhat questionable neighborhood because most of the prime rental units were snapped up in the early fall. Located at the edge of town, on a poorly lit street with few neighbors, my new digs left me edgy and cautious. I walked briskly to and from my car. My sleep was restless.

As much as I enjoyed the job, I felt isolated by living alone with little to no social life. Cold Minnesota weather, short daylight hours, and holidays away from home were the ingredients for sorrowful days and even longer nights.

I felt alone, lonely, down-in-the-dumps miserable. As though God had deserted me in this place and didn't love me anymore. Wrenching tears soaked my pillow most nights, too many to count. I even resorted to occasional forays to local pubs hoping to find potential friends. But this left me feeling hollow—a disastrous waste of time, and I felt abandoned.

Then God stepped in and took charge.

In May, I was at my co-worker's apartment, the two of us making weekend plans.

"Say, Jana, what about coming with me to my friend's lake cabin?" Diane asked.

Little did I know that God was planning for me, preparing me, setting me up to meet my future husband. When Randy and I met that fateful weekend, we felt an instant bond. A friendship took root and flourished into … more.

I could never have imagined a story in which I moved to a place out of my comfort zone (way out), where I knew no one, found and married the love of my life—and stayed throughout my entire career. A dear husband, three delightful children, a fulfilling career—only God could have orchestrated a dream life like mine.

It's a true story, a faith story, *my* story. A story I return to again and again to evaluate and mull and, in the end, offer praise and thanksgiving to The One who made it possible. It is the story that lifts and comforts me through widowhood.

I know that if He made it happen thirty-four years ago, He will do it again. He trained me decades ago to "be still and know" that He is God. He has not and will not leave me. I will wait for Him to unfold His plan for my life.

Sixty-five

Exactly where does a widow go to meet someone at this stage of her life? I ponder that question often in my alone time. If I were thirty years younger, the options would be endless. Wedding dances, out and about with friends on Friday night excursions, college functions, dormitory events? At this juncture, I recognize those scenes are past and passed.

So, where to start? On the bleachers? At the track? I've been there, attending kids' activities, but that era, too, is over and done. In the grocery store? Nope. Mostly I need food only for myself and trips there are few and far between. Church? I suppose, but I'm in and out quickly before and after each service. A larger community with a mega-church might afford an opportunity to join a small group of singles like me but that's not possible here, now.

In today's world, safety is a real concern when it comes to meeting a stranger. Frankly, I wrestle with this issue more than I expected; the angst it causes is real.

For Christmas, my sister Kathy got me a gag gift, *Dating After 50 for Dummies*. Together we read and chuckled and read and chuckled, until we doubled over with laughter at the suggestions and ideas to get back into the couple's scene.

Much of book was far-reaching and not my style even when I was younger and certainly not now. It was valuable as a light-hearted diversion, pure entertainment, and a jumping off point to discuss and brainstorm how I might proceed.

On the advice of close friends, I researched various social dating sites, never dreaming there were so many. My son's friend Katie helped design and edit my profile page. Her youthful and experienced technology viewpoint was helpful but left me hesitant and a tad wary.

For a while, I trolled the sites, timid and silent to maintain my privacy. I could see others but they couldn't see me. Bravely, I removed my private status and contemplated chatting with men whose interests dovetailed with my own. Contemplation was as far as I traveled.

Wow. That's all I can come up with to describe the initial experience. Dating has certainly changed from my high school and college days. Whatever happened to fate, anyway? Chance meetings? Or friends introducing friends? These sites make the awkward blind dates of my youth seem like a cakewalk. Or is that my self-confidence that has taken a nosedive? Who would want to date a woman my age, with three grown kids and years of wear and tear?

Needless to say, my online profile was short-lived. I put an end to perusing countless mirrored selfies of shirtless strangers. And hunting and fishing profiles, which are actually popular in my area of the country. I imagine the profile pictures of me with Max and me with my kids sparked some sort of speculation on the part of those perusing my online page. Like, really lady, move *on*. You're past the age of raising kids; you're single again. Live it up.

I've returned to the ever-hopeful ideal that someone,

somewhere, will introduce me to that special guy who connects with my faith and family life. My prayers and conversations with God continue as I ask for peace, provision, and patience to keep myself receptive to His call for my life.

This chapter of my life is still a blank page without structure or form, waiting to be conceptualized and written. But the waiting process finds me eager with anticipation and joy to imagine another life partner, another chance at love. God did it once and He will do it again when He's ready.

Sixty-six

When I was two years old and my brother Todd was three, we were playing outdoors until the chilly air drove us into the house. Sneaking into the kitchen, we decided to warm ourselves at the stove where Mom's fragrant soup bubbled on the range. We pulled open the oven door and stood on it to get closer to the heat from the boiling pot.

Our combined weight was too much. The stove tipped forward. Scalding soup cascaded down on us. Todd scrambled one way and I the other, making it impossible for Mom to reach for both of us at the same time. She caught hold of Todd's shirt and ripped it off to prevent the soup from burning deeper—while I ran and hid under the bed, scared of being scolded. By the time she found me, I was severely burned and in shock.

The aftermath is a haze of long bouts of hospital stays and multiple skin graft surgeries. The process stretched over the course of an entire year, most of the time spent hospitalized more than six hours from home. With sons age three and five and newborn daughter Kathy, Mom found it impractical to stay with me in the hospital.

I was a forlorn, frightened toddler with a chronic case of homesickness, too young to even know what the word meant. But it scarred me as surely as the burns, impacting my security, my psychological health for the remainder of my life.

Widowhood compounded those deep feelings that still mar me.

Homesick even now for Randy and our life together, I was, nevertheless, startled to feel those fingers of insecurity grasping at me under new circumstances.

More than a decade ago, my nieces, Kate and Annie, along with my sister and her husband started a non-profit foundation, All Day Fore Africa. ADFA strives to motivate kids to make a difference in the world. Their work in Rwanda, Africa, and the United States has been life changing and remarkable in so many ways. Each time they return from a trip, they tell rich stories about the lives impacted.

Repeatedly, Kathy asked me, begged me, pleaded with me to go with her, to accompany her on a trip to Africa. I listened. I honestly considered it, impressed and tempted to join them on one of their missions. But I could never fully picture myself leaving the country, being in a foreign country without my family. Traveling across the world. And to Africa, for goodness' sake.

I didn't even have a passport. So there. I couldn't go without a passport. Besides, it was too far and I would be too homesick.

In the fall of 2017, my son Tyler joined Kathy on an ADFA trip. "Mom, you have to go," he insisted between stories about all he had seen and done. "You just have to. You can do it."

Could I go? Could I really do it? I thought and prayed about the idea.

As luck would have it, airline tickets to Rwanda dropped to

a ridiculously low price. Obviously, I needed to really consider the trip. So in January, I purchased a ticket to visit Kibeho, Rwanda, with Kathy and six other women along with her parish priest, Father Jim.

Serious planning began early in 2018. At each meeting, I would admit my nervousness. We would discuss my latest concerns and, by the end of the meeting, I seemingly gained enough confidence to say, "I can do this."

Privately, Kathy and her daughters deflected each excuse I invented. Nothing I said fazed them as they persistently urged me to go, always remaining patient with my fears.

"You can do it, Jana. We'll be there with you."

The night before we were scheduled to leave, I phoned my sister.

"I can't do it, Kathy," I said. "Can I get my money back for the land package? I know I'm out the airline ticket, but that's fine."

But she wasn't going to let me off that easily. "What's wrong now, Jana? What is worrying you?"

We talked through my fears and concerns and I hung up with a renewed confidence. I went to bed that night repeating, "It's all okay. I can do this."

And I did.

I'm still not sure how or why, but I did. Prior to the trip, I expected a severe case of homesickness to strike far from home, in a foreign country. I expected the homesickness to be bad, as bad as it had been when Randy died. I certainly didn't want to revisit those emotions, to go back there and start over again.

But several days into the trip, while we were staying in the village of Kibeho, I had a life-changing moment. Kathy and I stayed awake too long, visiting and reminiscing about the day's events. Just as she was drifting off, I said, "Kathy, I can buy vacation time next year and with my PTO earned, we could come back for a whole month."

Her eyes flew open in disbelief. "Did I hear you right? You

want to travel here again?"

I nodded. Even I couldn't believe what I was saying! The gal who wanted so badly to stay home the night before leaving was now discussing ways to not only return in a year ... but to stay in Rwanda for a whole month?

That's when I realized that I had actually overcome the homesickness that had plagued me for decades. Oh, I missed my kids and my home—but *missing* home and *being* homesick were two separate feelings. The old familiar ache-in-my-chest-let-me-throw-up feeling never materialized to swamp and drown me.

God is faithful and God is good. He comforted me and protected me from homesickness so I could see His hand and serve in His mission while in Africa. What I thought I could never-ever-in-a-million-years overcome, God walked me through every step of the way.

Sixty-seven

Even after this epiphany experience, this miraculous melting away of my life-long struggle with homesickness, I still have days when I'm out of sorts. But the ache deep in my belly has dissolved. I take that as a sign I'm moving into a new season of my life. Past the homesickness into a freedom with no limits.

Debilitating grief no longer holds me back and keeps me from pressing forward. I journeyed through the other seasons by placing one foot in front of the other, taking steps to reach this new place by my own accord. All those single steps made me stronger and built confidence in my ability to thrive.

A quote jumped out at me on Facebook to capture the essence of what I had overcome: "The fears we don't face become our limits."

Homesickness had been a debilitating fear that limited me from reaching my potential solely because I hadn't confronted it. Randy's death forced me to revisit and reevaluate the limitations

I had placed on myself.

I faced them. I had no choice. Randy was not coming back. That unsettling feeling of homesickness had to be dealt with, or I would live with its limitation forever. For the sake of my kids and more so for my own sake, I had to free myself from this constraint.

My trek to Rwanda was so much more than a mission trip with my sister; it was an experience to push past the constrictions I had placed on myself after becoming a widow. It wasn't comfortable or easy, but today I find a new freedom and confidence in being able to venture from home. Although those reservations might creep into the corners of my mind again, I have more courage and strength to go places, to do things I never thought possible.

In Africa, we adopted a popular song "Waka Waka" by the Columbian singer Shakira, as our theme. A member of our group, America, taught all of us—including the children of Kibeho—a dance to the song, which enabled us to connect and bond with the students of the Children's Academy. Although language was a barrier, singing and dancing had no such boundaries, no such limits.

"Pick yourself up and dust yourself off and back in the saddle ...." The song melted deep into my heart as I reflected on my battle with homesickness and the limits I had put on myself.

Not coincidentally, I believe, I learned that Waka Waka is pidgin for "do it." It's that simple. It's that hard.

Sixty-eight

Spring, summer, autumn, winter. Four seasons. They come, they go.

Some seasons are longer than others and some are more welcomed than others, but they are all part of our life. Engrained with individual traits, temperatures, sights, smells, holidays, activities, advantages, disadvantages, each brings its own brand of excitement and anticipation. Often, we mark the passing of time in seasons.

From a calendar viewpoint, spring and fall have brought about the most significant metaphorical changes for my own life. For those of us who endure the deep cold of northern regions, spring is greeted with open arms.

Spring offers renewal. Fresh, fragrant air. Trees and plants budding out in all their exuberance. Birds and animals reproducing—squirrels, rabbits, geese …. Spring renews your hope and joy, your faith and expectation.

Summer, in all its simplicity, energizes. Stress evaporates as schedules loosen. Warmth saturates the outdoors and the lakes, which call you to the water to boat and ski and fish. Sunshine kisses your cheeks. Unpredictable storms startle you but are short-lived. You know for certain that each new dawn will bring more sun.

Fall, on the other hand, while rich in color is a season of loss. Trees shed their leaves, dead and brittle, in preparation for a time of dormancy, inactivity, stagnation. There is a loss of warmth, loss of outdoor activities and sports, loss of sunshine and socialization. Although showy and gorgeous, autumn is short-lived and has always been tough for me to navigate. Barren trees are a stark reminder of the long, dark winter ahead.

Winter for Minnesotans is long and challenging. Bone-numbing temperatures plunge to well below zero for weeks on end. Snow falls (often as much as 100 inches) and stays on the ground until spring. Like bears, we northerners hibernate, draw into ourselves. Social gatherings are sparse. Neighbors don't see neighbors. This solitary life is difficult and takes an extra ounce of patience to endure.

Here's what I've come to know: Life passes in seasons as well, some more painful than others. Understanding the calendar seasons helped me to unlock some of the mysteries of grief. Sorrow, too, is divided into time frames—some longer than others, some more painful than others.

Autumn: loss. When I said goodbye to Randy, our wedded life was no more. Although a huge measure of shock set in and hazes my sense of that period, absence and loss linger as the most vivid recollections. Warmth had been sucked from my being; the sun no longer spread its happy rays. And I was thrust, abruptly, into the next season of grief.

Winter: dormancy. For long, dark months I noticed little that occurred outside of me and my immediate family and our own unrecognizable situation. The world spun, an independent sphere, while I was unaware. What dominated the news channels? I had no clue. What did the headlines shout? I was oblivious. Oh, I watched. I read. But I was incapable of absorbing. My time and attention was fully engaged in demanding, day-to-day acts of survival.

Much like Minnesota winters when harsh conditions draw us indoors, I curled into myself trying to live without my beloved. While the storms raged outside, I fought for calm in the whirl of emotion, of hurt and heartbreak. Friends and family provided an element of warmth during this turbulent time. Still, I was grateful that a new season was on the horizon.

Spring: renewal and expectation. As I began to experience life outside my own head, I recognized the transitions waiting to happen. I learned to untangle myself from the past and embrace new beginnings. I accepted my state of singlehood as I loosened my grip on the beautiful, happy marriage Randy and I had shared.

The rest of my life, I acknowledged, was spread before me like a menu—and all the choices were up to me. Another season dawned.

Summer: action. I began to sit up and take notice of the rich blessings God placed right in front of me, around me. I learned to relax, to embrace the changes—and the opportunities—as they presented themselves. I rallied to my new norm, pulled up my big girl pants, and waded into the water.

This was the time to live again, for myself.

A re-entry stage followed. Meeting new people, exploring the world of friendships from a single woman's perspective—while taking note of how a change in circumstances creates a change in viewpoint which creates a change in opportunity which creates a change in *me.*

Gratitude—as a skillset and habit—became easier and more spontaneous, not something I had to work hard to feel and acknowledge. I more effortlessly savored the present rather than dwelling in the past.

Just like Mother Nature throws in unseasonable weather, a taste of winter surprises me in the middle of summer, but because I have traveled them all, I understand it's temporary. No season sticks around full-time.

Randy's untimely death has not been clearly revealed to me. Yet. I may have to wait until we meet in heaven to get a full explanation. And, trust me, it's top on my list to ask Jesus, "Why then? Why him?"

I may not understand, but my peace is no longer tied to an answer. My peace arrives along the paths God takes me.

Looking back, so many things and events pointed toward a preparation, of sorts, for Randy's departure. Those family vacations we took when fiscal responsibility suggested we shouldn't; we made memories to suffice for a lifetime of being Randy-less. Emily's new relationship with Mitchell when they visited frequently from Nashville; Mitchell got to know her dad. A "family" proposal, an early engagement party … more preparation to create memories and Randy's hearty approval for a wedding that would occur minus the father of the bride.

Why didn't Randy die on the side of the road the day he collapsed? I will always believe God graced us with those extra days to say our goodbyes, to spend time at his side during those last hours.

To prepare us.

The list of events is so long. And I couldn't always recognize them until after I weathered the seasons of grief.

The Bible reminds me to stay the course. "And let us not grow weary of doing good, for in due season we will reap, if we do not give up." Galatians 6:9 (ESV)

Sixty-nine

As I began to plan for my future, a verse from Jeremiah 29:11(NIV) etched itself into my mind and imprinted itself on my heart. "For I know the plans I have for you," declares the Lord, "plans to prosper you and not to harm you, plans to give you hope and a future."

How does traveling work for a fifty-something woman? How does retirement look from a single beach chair rather than a double?

Outside of traveling for work, I have not ventured out on my own yet, but I have researched and visited with other widows about how a person can feel safe and enjoy a trip on her own. Others do it successfully. I found a plethora of feasible options to consider. Mostly, I'm content to travel with my kids, sister, and friends. But, in time, I will give it a go.

Traveling with my now adult kids provides hours of pleasure and ample opportunities to create memories. We have made the unofficial commitment to take at least one family trip each year and our list of possible destinations appears endless.

Since I was a little girl, the Sipe family had gone on annual winter ski vacations to Montana and Colorado. One year the entire clan flew to Heavenly Valley in California for a weeklong Christmas ski vacation. Tyler, only two years old, ended up on the mountain between his dad's skis, learning to glide downhill.

After that experience, my young family adopted the tradition of downhill skiing, taking many mountain trips—an outing for all ages. No matter skill levels or abilities, everyone found something to enjoy.

Our kids were not slighted when it came to long distance travels, typically destinations we decided rather last minute. Our trips expanded their curious minds and exposed them to the world beyond their sheltered home in Breckenridge.

In one fell swoop, we had celebrated Emily's senior year of high school, which was also Matthew's last year in middle school and confirmation, which was also Tyler's senior year of college and my fiftieth birthday. Combining these milestones into one trip, Randy requested a few days of personal leave during the school year so we could surprise the kids with a long weekend to Disney World—indeed "the happiest place on earth!"

Emily maximized our time at the parks and Florida resort grounds by pushing us to start each day early and stretching them until long after my typical bedtime. By the time we flew home, we left no thrilling ride "un-ridden;" no themed, exotic food uneaten; no sprawling parade unwatched; no exhibition unvisited; no live Disney character unmet … at all four theme parks.

A whirlwind trip for sure, packed with laughter, strategic scouting of long lines, and using FastPass options to squeeze in yet another attraction. It was a Matterhorn memory to surpass any of the family vacations taken to that point.

As I reflect on the fortunate blessings we had as a family, I pray this will continue even after the much anticipated and prayed for grandchildren arrive.

Who knows? I might even branch out and travel some on my own.

Seventy

For Christmas in 2017 Tyler and Matthew gifted me with airline tickets to Breckenridge, Colorado, for a mother-son ski trip. Probably more in memory of their dad than about mom getting out, the time together was, nevertheless, priceless. Angel's Rest, the long blue diamond path, became my favorite.

The trip brought about a long discussed plan for all of us—a dream securely rooted years ago when Randy and I would tease about the hypothetical "someday."

Someday, when I die, I want my ashes spread at the lake ... in the mountains ... on the slopes ....

As vivid as though it was yesterday, I recalled the two of us discussing our deaths. What would happen to our bodies after we died? I asked him what he wanted. Burial? Cremation? He knew my personal preferences from previous discussions but had never shared his thoughts. This time, I pushed to find out.

"What would you want me to do?"

In typical Randy fashion, he said, "Jana, I won't be there so it really won't matter to me. You'll know what's best. I don't have a strong opinion either way."

Now our brief conversation suddenly seemed monumental.

During the afternoon after Randy died, Tyler and I had had a private conversation during which I shared the story of our discussion.

By then, Tyler had done some research and leaned toward cremation but knew it should be my decision. I consulted with the other kids and they, too, thought it was up to me. They would all support my decision. Pastor Terry and the funeral home answered my questions and continued to help me through my uncertainty.

I decided to think and pray before choosing.

I remembered when my parents were faced with the death of my sister in 1975. Where should her body lie to rest? And I remembered how, years later, they revisited their decision after they moved three hours away to central Minnesota. With no family left in the city where her marker stood, should they consider moving her grave?

I tried to put myself in my kids' shoes when, hopefully many years down the road, they would have to decide what to do with my body. Where would I want to rest permanently?

Cremation crept strongly into my mind. Was this best for him? And for us?

As the dark of night crept into my bedroom, a sense of peace swept over me. It was as though I heard Randy saying, "If that's what you want, it will be okay."

The next morning, I called the funeral home with my decision. We would have a casket and viewing at the prayer service, but immediately following the funeral they would prepare his body for cremation.

The urn holding Randy's ashes sits in the loft of the house in a specially etched memorial. In addition, the funeral home provided us with several separate containers of ashes to spread around *the lake ... the mountains ... the slopes* as we had teased years earlier.

And so it began.

During our mother-son ski trip to Colorado, we held a special ceremony on Angel's Rest. There we scattered a bit of Randy on the side of the mountain.

Freeing? Yes.

Emotional? Absolutely.

Fulfilling? Completely.

The following year we visited Sanibel Island during spring break and left a few ashes on the exact spot where Randy had built the engagement sandcastle for Emily and Mitchell.

Where the remainder of the ashes might land is yet to be decided, but most likely they will accompany us on some vacations in the coming years.

Because Matthew had once expressed a desire to be able to "visit" his dad if he ever wanted, I had had a memorial marker designed and placed at the cemetery between his parents' graves.

Each Memorial Day, I set a track shoe planter at Randy's marker, where a few of his ashes were buried.

But I know Randy is not in Sunnyside Cemetery. His soul is running with abandon in heaven.

His urn is on the shelf until I die and our ashes can be combined and buried together wherever the children determine. An image of the urn occasionally pops into my head, particularly when I drive to the lake each weekend. A little countryside cemetery sits just over the hill and seems peaceful, quaint—a perfect setting for a final resting place.

Perhaps we will rejoin there? It's a decision the kids will make someday. They'll know what's best. After all, I won't be there so it really won't matter to me!

Seventy-one

The first couple years of marriage had been difficult for
Emily and Mitchell as she continued to struggle with her PTSD.
Consequently, her rollercoaster of emotions had led them to a
life-changing decision: In January of 2017, they made the painful
decision to move back to Minnesota to be closer to family. On a
personal level, having her nearby had calmed some of my mother-
fears and rejuvenated our family time.

I witnessed how their move to nearby Minneapolis was
very much God's plan; it gave her space and time to heal and
regain strength.

But by the fall of 2018, I sensed Emily was getting
anxious about her future and their married life. Our daily phone
conversations held a wary undertone.

How long until they decide to return to Nashville?
I wondered.

In September of that year, Emily and Mitchell traveled to

Tennessee for a conference at The Belonging Co, the mega-church they used to attend. The conference did wonders for their faith and their marriage even as it stirred Emily's heart and gave her a renewed sense of strength to return to complete her dreams.

An email in October confirmed my dread. They decided to move back.

Even in my heartbreak, I understood that it was time. Her years of fighting to conquer the PTSD had come full circle and her hard work had paid off. She was healthy again; our Emily was back.

I wrestled with my emotions. Which would I rather have? Healthy Emily living in Nashville or struggling Emily living in misery in Minnesota? I knew my answer, a clear choice winner. With the blessing of her therapist, she was ready for the next big thing in her life.

A deep sadness swept over me as I processed the words on the computer screen. I didn't want to influence their decision with my selfish desire to keep them in Minnesota, with the aching, oh-so-familiar homesickness pressing in on me. I waited until the next day to email back.

Emily, I've read your letter, actually several times. The first time, I had to stop to wipe the tears… the second wasn't much easier. This was for many reasons, but mainly because I know what you are writing is hard. I know this is not easy for you and I want you to know that I love you and there is nothing that you can do to stop me from loving you.

The news to move back to Nashville has been, for the most part, my worst fear … just like it was in 2013 when you moved there the first time. We survived back then and we will survive again.

With cars and a U-Haul truck stuffed to the top, we made the trek back to Nashville in January, settling them into their new home on Pawnee Trail. Conflicting emotions surfaced as I drove away. Grief over yet another change. Worry at the distance separating us. Fear that she would slip back into depression. But I dug deep for some of the resilience so recently acquired. I was only a phone call, a Facetime conversation, a plane ride away.

As I sat in church Sunday morning, God reassured me. *Jana, your girl is better. She's overcome her big obstacle.*

Through blurry eyes, I followed along as the pastor read from the same passage our family had clutched at over the past four years. The same Run with Randy verse that had spoken loudly to each of us about our faith and our trust in God.

"Let us run with perseverance the race marked out before us." Hebrews 12:1 (NIV)

Seventy-two

My secret dream and prayer? To connect with Randy's organ transplant benefactors. Early on, I wrote a letter to each, describing the amazing man who gifted their chance at new lives. I continued to acknowledge their yearly anniversaries with notes of encouragement and well wishes. This was my way to ask, plead, pray that I received letters in return—wanting to learn about the changes they experienced since being freed from their prior limitations.

Four years, letters each year and … nothing.

One bright day, I parked my Acadia in the garage and, with purse and backpack in hand, strolled to the mailbox to collect the usual junk mail and utility bills. I pulled out a surprisingly oversized envelope and immediately recognized the logo.

LifeSource! This is odd, I thought. Typically, their letters, solicitations, and invitations were compact or small. Curious, I rushed back into the garage, tossed aside the extra mail, and slit open the envelope.

I pulled out a letter—along with a legal-sized envelope hand-addressed to *Jana.*

Without bothering to read the cover letter, I ripped open the second envelope. A handwritten note from one of the kidney recipients!

My heart skipped a beat and my hands trembled as I sank onto the step, eyes racing down the ordinary, college-ruled paper.

A male recipient … lived and worked on a farm his entire life … looking forward to retiring to his lake home … northern Minnesota ….

He filled in other details about his life, but it was the closing signature that caught and held my attention. He signed his name: *Randy.*

This Randy lives on because of your Randy's gift of life, he added.

I was overcome with emotion, feeling like I had reconnected with my husband through another Randy.

Warmth flooded through my veins. I sat on the garage steps for a long time, thinking, praying, and thanking God. I had finally received a response, a heartening response, about the change and blessing Randy's gift had wrought in one man's life.

Carefully refolding the letter, I decided to save and share it with the kids.

Just as we had for years, we gathered at the lake on Father's Day. After church and brunch, I suggested we take their dad's boat for a spin in his honor. The kids clambered onto the *Larson.* I joined them, paused, and pulled out the letter.

One man's simply written words of gratification swept over us. Fresh tears of poignant joy coursed down our cheeks. Our Randy lived on!

Beyond
A NEW NORMAL
· ·

Seventy-three

The familiar children's song, " *I have the joy, joy, joy, joy down in my heart. Down in my heart to stay!*" often rings through my mind. The catchy ditty fills and feeds me as I fight the good fight of keeping joy in my heart.

Where does it go? Why is it so hard as we "adult" to keep our joy burning as brightly as when we were kids at Bible school?

Understandably, life throws curve balls our way. Some have punched me squarely in the face. That's when I've had to remind myself that joy is lost only if I allow it. I can be intentional about keeping it.

I *choose* to choose joy.

Hard as it was, it's becoming more natural for me as I paddle through this river of mourning.

Thommi Odom, a professional career coach, says, "Joy is defined many different ways. It is different from happiness in that it is more than just a state of mind. It is bigger than an emotion.

Joy is housed in our hearts and souls."

It's that sense of peace that passes all understanding. It's the inner knowing of and belief in something greater than anything else my eyes alone can see.

The Dalai Lama defines it this way: "Joy is inside not outside. It's not in spite of adversity, it's because of adversity. Adversity can point us to a profound sense of gratitude. True joy and struggling may actually be tied together."

Joy and struggle? How can that be? Perhaps he means that without deep sorrow one can't truly appreciate profound joy. So, time after time, I practice gratitude in the midst of my utter sadness and despair. This allows me to feel joy rather than sorrow.

As my faith increases and my spiritual life grows, I discover a deeper satisfaction and ease of heart. Could it be that losing Randy (adversity) actually causes me to find more contentment (joy)?

Long before I knew *I* needed to change my view about joy, Randy and I started a family ritual. To temper our young children's (ages three to ten) constant "gimme, gimme, and gimme more" attitude, we instigated a nightly ritual of expressing thankfulness—hoping to help them appreciate and find contentment in what they already had.

At the dinner table each evening that year, we asked the kids to tell us something they were grateful for that day. Ranging from the commonplace "I was happy we got to play outside for recess," to the ornery "I'm glad I didn't cry when Daddy yelled at me," to the uncooperative "Matthew is not finding anything today to be happy about"—their comments brightened the room and were duly recorded in *The Berndt Happy Times Journal*.

Especially memorable is first grader Emily's offering the day of her new haircut: "I'm happy cuz now I finally look like Hallie Parker," (her favorite character in the remake of the movie, "The Parent Trap.")

It was awkward at first, but the kids had some fun with it. When I was rushed or forgot one of them would say, "Hey what about being thankful?"

That simple exercise paid big dividends for our family over the course of several years.

As I reread the journal, I see how our family dynamics blossomed, how our gratitude grew, from a year focused on blessings. Who knows, perhaps someday *The Berndt Happy Times Journal* will make its way back into circulation at the dinner table of one of my kids.

With all my heart, I believe what author Matthew Kelly writes, "Gratitude is a sure path to joy."

And so I continue to ask myself the same question Randy and I posed to Tyler, Emily, and Matthew so many years ago: What brought you joy today?

Cathey, I think. *Cathey brings me joy. Every time she's at my house, I'm filled to the top.*

Cathey was my Mother's Day gift nearly thirty years ago. Busy working fulltime and raising our first child, Randy and I were breaking a sweat to stay ahead of hectic demands and still keeping our household running in a clean, efficient manner.

Weekdays were filled with jobs, cooking, bedtime routines, preparation for the next day. Weekends were consumed with cleaning bathrooms and changing sheets and doing laundry and shopping for groceries and planning meals and volunteering at church ... I was drained.

With Mother's Day approaching, Randy begged for gift ideas. Freda popped into my mind. When I was growing up, my mom had Freda—who arrived every week to help with the household work. She kept my mom's life in balance and I craved that same semblance of order.

Without missing a beat, I said, "I'd like someone or something to give me my Saturdays back. What about checking into the Merry Maids?"

Randy found Cathey, household savior and now my dear, dear friend. She pours love into our home. She relieves my burdens, makes me smile, and fills me to the brim.

About ten years into her bi-weekly appearance at the Berndt house, Cathey suffered a disabling back injury, forcing her to quit. Pity for her and her pain quickly evolved into pity for myself. Saturdays had reverted to a torturous ending to my week and directly impacted my crabbiness. Something had to give.

Randy to the rescue!

He printed little slips of paper with household tasks: Empty the wastebaskets. Dust the furniture. Clean the kitchen floor. The five of us took turns drawing slips and tackling the assigned jobs. The house wasn't Cathey-perfect, but it passed the Jana test.

A few years later, Cathey lost her husband to a heart attack. Several months after his funeral, we bumped into each other at the neighborhood grocery store. After chatting a bit, she asked, "Have you found someone to take care of your house?"

"Not yet," I sheepishly replied. "I haven't been able to find someone to love and care for us like you did all those years."

It's not like we hadn't tried, there just wasn't another Cathey. We had hired one lady, but several days before she arrived, I called and cancelled. No one could replace my Merry Maid.

"You've all been on my mind," Cathey confided. "I've thought about reaching out and asking to come back."

Her back injury had healed. She felt much better, and she really missed our family.

"Seriously? That would be an answer to prayer!" Joy had arrived—in the midst of our struggles.

The next Thursday night, as was our routine, we straightened (or cleaned as the kids accused) the house, ready for the doorbell to ring early Friday morning. Max raced to greet her. Cathey was back! So was my joy.

Only a short time later, I would join Cathey as a widow, cementing our bond in yet another way. The gift that keeps on giving.

• • • • • • • •

As I intentionally sought joy, I spent more and more time with people who exhibited positivity. You know the type, those people who make you laugh when you want to cry. Those who see the good rather than the bad.

Nothing lifted my spirits like an afternoon with Emma and Cate, Marcia's three- and five-year-old granddaughters. Their youthful antics made me laugh. Their unconditional love melted my heart. And they made my heart long for the day when I might be officially called Grandma Jana.

Day to day, I sought opportunities to connect and grow friendships with women who shared professional challenges similar to mine. Our "women and faith" group was a God-sent gift.

After my friend Colette lost her husband, a small group of us surrounded her to offer support and carry some of her burdens. We gathered at each other's homes over lunch, connecting. All of us held leadership roles in the community yet we had no agenda outside of uplifting conversation and quality time together.

Each time we met, I was fed with much more than food. I felt as though they listened and *heard*. Their stories and counsel enlightened me. And I felt loved merely by the time each busy woman committed to our group.

• • • • • • • •

As a friend who talked me off the cliff multiple times during my grieving, Marcia noticed it first. "You seem more at peace these days."

Knee-jerk reactions come less often. Negativity takes a back seat to my sunnier outlook. Quick anger joins him there. I am more likely to act rather than react, to temper my anger with a patient, well-thought response.

Worries that once kept me awake at night seem trivial.

Anxiousness evaporates. I have a new benchmark: If it isn't a death sentence, then it isn't bad enough to lose sleep over.

Life is better balanced and my emotions even-keeled.

When my boss asked me to attend a meeting at his office in Alexandria, a bit of an atypical work situation, speculative thoughts toyed with my attention. *I wonder if there is more to this meeting? Is my job at risk?*

Once again that old enemy, Worry, appeared to demand attention. Now without a spouse to confide in, I took my concern to God.

"Please," I prayed, "take this anxiety and dread. Remove them from my heart. Please, give me peace."

I dug deep and shoved the worrisome thoughts to the back of my mind.

When the meeting day arrived, my boss asked, "Jana, would you like to check out the new juice bar down the street?"

Over lunch, our conversation felt short, a tad forced, out of sync compared to our typical interactions. When he seemed a tad nervous, my antenna shot up.

He has something to announce. I wonder if I'm losing my job?

First, the good news. My job was solid, my performance at work was not in question. Our company, he confided, was going through a change, a change that impacted my job, reporting relationship, and—ultimately—the location of my office.

Then, the tough news. This change ran smack into the middle of my plans, owning the new lake place and being nearer to family in Alexandria. My new role would take me on the road west and north, no longer south and east of Breckenridge. This was a low blow; I had been working for years toward getting my job closer to Alexandria. My community involvement and newly formed friendships would have to be put on hold.

Although I felt disbelief and disappointment, I no longer had those feelings of anxiousness over the impending disarray of my life. Instead, I encountered … peace and acceptance. I saw the positives rather than the negatives I more often focused on in the past. It was refreshing.

Joy in the midst of sadness had proven itself. That valuable lesson rang loudly in my ears. Death is permanent. Everything else is just temporary.

Seventy-four

Mother Teresa described J-O-Y as J-esus, O-thers, and Y-ou. In that order. When you put Jesus first and invest in other people before yourself, you are filled with joy.

This isn't to say you shouldn't take care of yourself, ensure that your needs are met. During the last few years, it was mandatory that I focus on inward healing, taking care of myself and family. However, I'm discovering that true and lasting joy requires me to lay down my pride and allow Jesus to love others through me, which often means setting aside my grumblings and agendas.

At times when I didn't feel well or experienced debilitating sadness, I figured out that I had displaced the J-O-Y order. Sometimes I had it backwards: Y-O-J. An adjustment to the letter order is all it took and my attitude would do an immediate flip-flop. It's not as difficult as you might imagine.

Figuratively speaking, I steal a page from *The Berndt Happy Times Journal* by starting my day with gratitude. Thanking

Jesus for my blessings, naming "them one by one." Trust me, even on the blackest days, the blessings are there. Start … and the list just keeps growing as you focus on Him rather than the negatives you are enduring.

When I do good for others, I keep the "J" in first place. I visit a friend in the hospital or nursing home, lunch with someone who doesn't get out much, meet with another widow to share stories, confide fears, and offer support.

Three years after Randy died, I had a unique opportunity through the bank. A client's thirty-something husband tragically collapsed and died. Like me, she felt too young to face life without her spouse. It was my privilege to help this shattered, bereaved woman.

I understood and empathized with her state of shock. Her utter disbelief. Her floundering mind. At our meeting, I gingerly walked her through some basic information to alleviate her immediate concerns. All the while, I envisioned the long, rocky road ahead of her. My heart ached for all she must yet experience and overcome, but I did my best to keep a positive tone as I encouraged her to get through each moment, to take small steps forward. Strangers before that day, we bonded as widows.

That night, I crawled into bed in utter joy. Not because I was pleased with myself, but because God had used me to help another grieving soul find her way through her suddenly broken, beaten up world.

A few months later I sat in the bank, at the same table, across from a client-friend who sought my advice. His son—a father of five, including an infant—had recently lost his young wife to a sudden, unexplained infection. He came to me seeking insight, trying to glean anything he could about the grieving process, to help his mourning son.

How did you handle this? How did you view this? How did this or that go for you? He grasped desperately at anything he might use to ease his son's pain.

Something, something humbling but exciting, was unfolding before my eyes. Was it possible God was using my circumstance to help others? Was there a greater purpose in Randy's death after all? Was there value in my pain? New purpose to my life?

I am certainly not a grief expert, a mental health counselor, or a saint as I continue to meet with and help those suffering souls intersecting my life. Strangely, satisfactorily, perhaps even selfishly, I heal a tiny bit more with each encounter as we share our mutual heartbreak.

The "O" in J-O-Y plays out in God's mysterious ways.

Seventy-five

I have told you this so that my joy might be in you and your joy might be complete. John 15:11 (NIV)

Recognizing the Author of joy, true joy, is a lasting source of strength and peace that carries me through my hardest days. The million-dollar question is: How do you find joy in the midst of suffering?

One of the most life-changing lessons I've learned is that it's not about finding; it's about mindset. It's about attitude. No matter your circumstance, no matter what life throws at you, no matter what somebody does or says to you, you choose your response.

Bad news lurks on every street corner. Struggle and contention and bitterness—joy's polar opposites—seek a stronghold in every person. Pick up a newspaper, listen to the nightly news, linger in the coffee shop. You'll be hammered by negativity. But no matter what you see or say, no matter what you listen to and process, it is up to you whether you swallow and digest it all. You choose how you react.

Although more sporadic and further apart, I am still plagued with my share of why-me-this-isn't-fair moments. This internal smack talk doesn't improve my situation any. I continue to practice replacing poor-me thoughts with I'm-so-blessed thoughts. The fight is real. But a positive approach is absolutely more beneficial. For me *and* those around me.

I still really, really, *really* miss Randy and I am still really, really, *really* sad at times. But the difference at this point? I don't get mad, angry, or bitter. I push back when those pesky pity parties threaten to interfere. Emotions—the negative and the positive—are all fleeting.

When I find myself missing Randy, I allow myself to miss him. For a short while. I spend a brief time thinking about him and what I miss about him. This makes it easier to be thankful for who he was and how he touched my life so that it is less about me and the unfairness of it all—and more about the gift he was to me.

Ultimately, my sorrow is no longer crippling as I channel my inner strength to find gratitude in the ongoing struggle to place joy foremost.

Seventy-six

I am challenged by a recurring question: "How is Run with Randy going?"

"It's going well," I always reply. But I always wonder if there is a better way to respond.

The Run with Randy movement began on a whim at Randy's bedside and continues to evolve. With help from friends Janet and Ann, it grew to include tee-shirts that continue to broaden the impact.

The first year, we asked people to send photos of the Run with Randy experiences. We delightedly posted their shots, taken in various countries during a vast variety of activities and serving all kinds of causes.

What began in 2014 as a way to remember Randy has become much more purposeful to friends, family, and others.

For athletes in our group, RWR literally means they have Run with Randy. They wear their RWR shirts as they gallivant across the countryside or endure the grueling miles of a marathon or simply take a meditative walk. Some shared their runs, which we posted on the Run with Randy Facebook page.

Randy runs, vicariously, all over the country and even the world!

Every message or text from anyone who runs in Randy's memory warms my heart. I continue to receive pictures, too many to post, each representing much more than simple exercise. I feel the runners' deep devotion to a man who inspired them to do something extraordinary with their lives.

A marathon runner in Antarctica. Kids participating in their first 5Ks in Randy's memory. Groups sporting their RWR tee-shirts for a cause—while keeping Randy in their hearts. One group of twenty-four runners had never even met Randy; they had read our family's story and wanted to do something in his honor.

For others RWR means they did something out of the ordinary or completed a goal. Each runner has the Randy Berndt spirit of hard work, dedication, not giving up, and doing their best at whatever they set out to do.

Many have taken their tee-shirts on trips to places Randy had never been. Trips at sea, trips to national parks, trips to foreign countries. Reordered several times, nearly 2,000 tees roam the globe.

Some runners have already exhibited years of devotion; others have seen it as a singular moment in time. I've witnessed group efforts and individual accomplishments. Randy's character, values, and personality left a mark on each one of us.

For me, Run with Randy offers a unique purpose: Every day I vow to work toward creating a life pleasing to God, just like Randy did.

Run with Randy put me on a path that God orchestrated. I didn't choose this life, nor did I choose the events of these past years. But RWR helps me live a life that moves beyond my sorrow, step by step!

Seventy-seven

"Change is the only constant.... the variable is how we deal with it." ~ meauthentic.com

So.

Norm left and my world is no longer normal.

The road I've traveled has been long. Difficult. Finding my way and purpose without Randy has taken time. It has taken perseverance. And it has taken courage. As I floundered day by day, it was often hard to note any progress. My steps were tiny.

Yet, in a strange way, these years were rewarding ... rewarding because I've grown in faith as well as confidence. I'm comfortable with who I am without Randy.

As I reflect over the past years I see how everything happened on time, in God's time. God was at my side the entire trip, stretching, encouraging, loving, and pushing me to a life with Him as guide. He nudged and challenged me to become the very best version of myself. The person He created me to be.

I learned to trust Him in newer and deeper ways— even on the darkest days, even at my lowest points. I developed an unwavering trust I might never have refined without this journey of loss. Although it's been the hardest work I've ever encountered, God brought me through it to heights beyond belief: a fresh perspective full of hope, filled with gratitude, and overflowing with faith.

And I'm settled in my new norm: life without my dear husband, untangled, abundant with joy, and appreciation for the blessings I continue to receive.

The website meauthentic.com posted: "Dealing with change is never easy; unfortunately, it's unavoidable. As humans, it is only natural for us to want things to remain 'as-is' when we are in our comfort zones. But sometimes either things happen or we make choices that completely change our daily routines."

This resonates with me as I watch my kids move on with their lives and leap into adulthood. They, too, encountered struggles as they fought to find their new norm, and they've grown throughout the process. They are survivors, just like their mother. Each has matured and developed their own kind of resilience on their own timeframe and in their own way.

Tyler's move to Minneapolis after college graduation proved to be a good decision for his career and social life. I see so many of his dad's characteristics: his unquenchable thirst for knowledge, his aptitude for learning, his patient demeanor, his unfailing kindness. Randy would be so proud of his firstborn son. Tyler continues to run, often with his dad or friend David in mind. When we're together, Tyler often shares memories of Randy and quotes his dad's advice.

Bolstered by a growing career and a strong group of friends, he is happy and content. In his spare time he travels, often to fascinating international locations. With his love for flying and experiencing life beyond Minneapolis, I'm sure to have an eager travel companion as the occasions present themselves.

Emily and Mitchell are finishing what they set out to do years ago. Once again in Nashville, they have restarted their careers and ministry in their local church. With established home businesses—Mitchell in technology, my daughter as an online fashion stylist, they strive to balance work and family life, ongoing challenges for every millennial family. The excitement of first-time home ownership casts a bright glow on their future.

Emily inherited her dad's love of reading and writing, so she often journals at her desk or curls up on the couch to read the latest Christian self-help book. Her beauty and poise reminds me of photographs of Randy's mom, Vera, who had a broad collection of books.

Of my three kids, Matthew probably exhibits the most personal growth from the earth-shattering loss of his dad. Faced with taking on adult responsibilities as a high schooler—solely by his own choice, he manfully shouldered the mantel of household caretaker and the onerous tasks that accompany homeownership. He did it without complaint.

The results are a maturity that far surpasses other young men his age.

As I prepare to watch him walk across the stage to receive his college diploma, I catch my breath in pride for his academic accomplishments. Equally impressive to this grateful mom is his strength of character. Life has dealt him a harsh blow, but he rose to the challenge and became a strong person in spite of it.

Where he'll go from here is yet to unfold, but I see a bright future for him and his someday family. He's my last hope of a child who follows his grandfather, uncle and mom into the banking industry. As his life unfolds, it's becoming a real possibility.

Seventy-eight

At a community leaders' support luncheon, we were offered a challenge by Pastor Jen, who suggested we join her in a "Star Word" devotion. Each woman would receive a word chosen by another pastor friend of hers. The words—prayed over prior to being assigned—would become ours for a year, a guidepost and theme for our lives.

Evangelism. Gentleness. Sympathy. Humility. The women received their words with open hands and open minds.

My word was … education.

Education? Really? It seemed so different from the others. Why that word? Did it somehow relate to Randy being a teacher?

I sought scripture verses that included "education" and was stunned at the endless references in the Bible. I prayed, asking God to reveal His hows, whys, and whats for this word as it applied to my life.

I explored the idea that I should educate and help other

widows through their grief and share with them helpful tips on how to survive widowhood. But that seemed rather lofty and illogical as I worked fulltime and certainly wasn't eager to hit the pavement to speak about my sorrow and experience.

Then, over several weekends, I went back to the blog I had started in 2014 and began writing my thoughts, my story of loss, the lessons I'd learned, and how I found joy amidst my agony.

The proverbial light bulb lit up and I wondered: *Maybe … maybe I'm supposed to write a book?*

A book was a logical vehicle to share how one frightened, uncertain widow survived. Survived and flourished. If my story could help others with their losses, it would be worth my effort and time to publish.

So education it was.

Drawn from my blog entries, journals, texts, and Facebook posts, the bits and pieces became a manuscript, and a highly recommended editor, Carol, smoothed the rough edges and organized it into something logical.

Only God knows what will happen next, where it will land, whether it will educate and inspire those who deign to read it. Perhaps it will help them move beyond their own grief.

For our family, the writing process was an education and a measure of therapy. I found how healing it was to write and rewrite these stories—despite floods of tears, prevailing angst, and an overall sense of unsettledness. But as months passed and edits were incorporated and massive changes made, I was able to dig deeper to release thoughts and stories so entwined in my heartstrings.

Tyler, with his attention to detail and innate writing ability, encouraged and guided me until I could see this dream's potential. His input helped me tell my story in a way that others might find joy and hope in times of great loss.

Although he didn't openly share with me how this book impacted his life, I sensed that he, too, found immense value in the writing. Emails, texts, and phone conversations abounded between us until one day he suggested we meet in Alexandria to discuss his suggestions and changes. It pleased me to see how much he cared about the project.

Through reading and proofing early versions of the manuscript, Emily's heart stirred. She received clarity and vision for her life and marriage. She discovered how far she had come and how much stronger she was having lived through this devastation—which enabled her to pull up stakes and return to Nashville.

Matthew's silence during this flurry of writing and rewriting tells me he isn't quite ready to read the story, to digest the emotions that accompany it. Privy to the many discussions and late night talks and piles of proofs strewn across the kitchen, he probably knows more about the book than I even suspect.

At times, I still feel like I'm climbing a towering mountain. The climb is long, the climb is hard, and the climb is invigorating. Some places are steep. Others are slippery and unpredictable. A few are flat and easier to navigate.

In some places, I need to stop. Catch my breath. Replenish my energy. I've come this far and there's no going back, so I put one foot in front of the other and press forward. I can't see the peak, but I know it's ahead somewhere.

Every mountain climber knows the payoff, the reward for sweat and effort and agony, is the ultimate view from the peak. From there, you can look out and see where you started, the trail you traveled, how high you climbed—and the view beyond.

From that high advantage, you know this for certain: You did it! You accomplished what you set out to do. You conquered the challenge placed before you.

I'm still climbing this massive mountain of grief. But I know I will finally reach the top. And—when I do—what a mountaintop moment that will be!

Acknowledgements

I dreamed of sharing my story to comfort and help others who find themselves widowed. If *Finding Norm* gives hope and encouragement to those drowning in grief, then I will have accomplished my goal. But this project surprised me; I discovered that the process of putting words to my memories and emotions holds healing powers I never imagined.

As I reflect on the many months of writing, editing, rewriting—and praying for God's guidance, I am eternally grateful to the many who stood by me along the way.

Where do you begin to thank those who propped you up, who lifted you? Those who patiently read, reread, and provided honest feedback? Who listened (even when they were tired)? Who encouraged when you needed it most? Who stood by you as friends in the truest sense?

Humbled by their actions, I still want to try. And so I offer my most sincere appreciation to this partial list of my incredible team:

My children, Tyler, Emily, and Matthew: for giving me the rewarding title of Mom. Their love, support, and encouragement throughout the years, and especially during the writing of this book, is a blessing I cannot put into words.

My parents, Gene and Marilyn Sipe: for raising me in a family to whom they taught the real meaning of love and commitment. They set the bar high for their Sipe descendants and led us by example—their enduring sixty-two-year marriage. They continue to be my rock.

The Lesnars, Kathy, Jim, Kate, and Annie: for bolstering us every step of the way and modeling a loving family. Weekends would have been unbearable if it hadn't been for our Buck Saw Lodge outings.

Friends and family: for shouldering my late night rants and early morning tears. They carried me through the darkest days of my life and still stand at my side.

My editor, Carol: for stretching me to my limits and pushing me to finish what I started. Her faith in the project and vision of what it could become was a God-send.

My early readers: for rallying behind me and urging me to take my manuscript to the next level. Dad corrected grammar and eliminated the commas I so badly use. Mom survived late night hours through my first draft. My kids and sister offered advice and endless discussion about what should or should not be included. Friends read the earliest, roughest versions and courageously provided feedback and advice along the way.

People near and far: for sustaining me even when I wasn't aware. Their prayers and love strengthened me.

This labor of love certainly "took a village" to get it to publication. And I am eternally grateful.
F. Scott Fitzgerald summed it up best, "There are all kinds of love in this world, but never the same love twice." Writing about the once-in-a-lifetime love I shared with Randy has deepened my belief in God and His amazing plan that brought us together.